Pioneers of Flight

by
Henry T. Wallhauser

Illustrations
by Jack Woodson

HAMMOND®
INCORPORATED

Acknowledgments

Picture credits — The Boeing Company: 90. Brown Brothers: 18 (Cayley design), 25, 29, 31 (H. Quimby), 58, 73, 75, 77. Culver Pictures, Inc.: 18 (Lilienthal glider), 81, 89. Douglas Aircraft Co., Inc.: 90. C. H. Gibbs-Smith: 15 (Da Vinci sketch & Da Vinci ornithopter), 18 (Pénaud design). National Cash Register Co.: 20 (Wright motor). *The New York Times:* 87. North American Rockwell Corp.: 91. *Scientific American Supplement, 1910:* 18 (Maxim steam plane). Smithsonian Institution, National Air and Space Museum: 9, 10, 11, 12, 15 (Da Vinci portrait), 16, 17 (Baldwin photo), 18 (Cayley portrait), 20 (Wright plane), 22, 27, 30, 31 (White on street before White House), 33, 34, 35, 36, 37, 40, 45, 47, 48, 51, 52, 56 (Patrick & Mitchell), 59 60, 61, 64, 65, 67, 71, 80, 82, 85, 86. U.S. Air Force: 90 (Bell X-1). U.S. Army Air Force National Archives: 23, 32, 56 (pilots, 11th Bomb. Sq.) U.S. Signal Corps National Archives 17 (Baldwin dirigible), 26, 38. U.S. War Dept. General Staff National Archives: 41.

Text credits — Quotation on page 51 from *Rickenbacker,* by Capt. Edward V. Rickenbacker. Prentice Hall, Inc. Quotation on page 55 from *Memoirs of World War I,* by William Mitchell. Random House, Inc. Quotation on page 80 from *The Airmail — Jennies to Jets,* by Benjamin P. Lipsner. Wilcox and Follett.

Contents

1
1903-The Pivotal Year

"God didn't intend man to fly," the saying went. "If He had, He would have given him a set of wings." Such was the sober judgment of the man in the street on the record of flying attempts as the 20th century began. True, men had been drifting through the skies in balloons for more than a hundred years. Small and primitive model aircraft had floated for brief distances before they sputtered out and died. Gliders also had been built that could sail off hilltops and alight safely upon the earth. And there had even been reports during the 1890's of fixed-wing flying machines leaving the ground under their own power for short hops of a few feet. But none of these efforts added up to the age-old dream of flying — the ability of man to take off and keep himself in the air with such controlling factors as wings and motive power.

Nineteenth century aerial experiment was littered with crackpots and cranks. Devices which seemed as weird then as they seem now flapped, fluttered, clanked and coughed their way to utter failure. At the same time,

though, serious and dedicated men were trying to prove flight was possible. Europe was the scene of numerous experiments, several of which stand as landmarks along the path toward sustained flight.

At the dawn of the 20th century attention suddenly shifted to America. There, three men prepared to challenge the skies for the prize that had so long eluded humanity. Two of them were obscure bicycle builders from the Midwest. The third was an eminent scientist whose work in astronomy and the study of the sun had already gained him an international reputation. Ironically, it was the Wright brothers from Dayton, Ohio, who were to triumph. And it was the scientist, Professor Samuel P. Langley, who was to fail. The year of their great attempts was 1903. It marked the beginning of modern aviation history.

Samuel Pierpont Langley was well into middle age when he tackled the problem of flight in earnest. Behind him were many years of scientific achievement as a first-rate contributor in the field of astronomical

Opposite
Langley's steam-operated model *Aerodrome*

Below
White-bearded Prof. Langley and
his assistant and pilot, Charles Manly

research. In the year 1886, when he was
52 years old, Prof. Langley listened intently
to a speech in Buffalo, N.Y., on the flight of
soaring birds. As a boy in Massachusetts he
had been fascinated by the motion of winged
creatures in the skies. The talk, given at a
meeting of professional scientists, reawakened
that old interest. Now this somewhat stiff
and formal man with intelligent eyes and
stout figure embarked upon a painstaking
study of the possibility of man's flight.
Building a revolving table equipped with 30-
foot arms and a 10-horsepower steam engine
he attempted to gauge the effects of aerodynamic lift upon swiftly moving surfaces.
Although his results varied, Langley could
conclude by 1891 that flight at high speeds
" . . . is not only possible but within the reach
of mechanical means which we now possess."

The white-bearded scientist next moved on
to more sophisticated tests by first using a
rubber-band-powered model and then building
steam-powered models as large as 16 feet in
length. Langley called these models "Aerodromes" (a combination of Greek words
meaning *air runner*) and catapulted them
from a houseboat anchored in the Potomac
River near Washington, D.C. With his *Aerodrome No. 6* he achieved a miniature triumph
in November 1896 when the machine shot
off the houseboat and traveled three-quarters
of a mile before it ran out of fuel. The
world took little notice, however, and Langley
seemed to be satisfied with his accomplishment. He wrote soon after, "I have brought
to a close the portion of the work which
seemed specially mine — the demonstration
of the practicability of mechanical flight —
and for the next stage, which is the commercial and practical development of the
idea, it is probable that the world may look
to others."

Though he did not realize it at the time,
Langley's most ambitious projects were still

to come. After his model *Aerodrome* experiments he had written of the military potential of flying machines, predicting that their
use as mobile observation posts could change
the whole nature of warfare. Two years after
he had called his aerial work finished, America went to war with Spain. Langley soon
received a request from President William
McKinley asking him to resume his experiments, as well as a promise from the War
Department of $50,000 to help carry them
out. At first the ex-professor of astronomy
hesitated. By now he was the head of the
famed Smithsonian Institution in Washington
and very busy with his duties there. But he
finally agreed, believing that the building of
a man-carrying plane would be of great
aid to his nation.

The craft he produced after five years of
research was an outsized *Aerodrome* 55 feet
long, 48 feet wide and with a wing area of
1,040 square feet. Although it hewed closely
to the design of its smaller predecessors, it
differed radically in the power it used. Steam
had propelled the model *Aerodromes,* but

The Manly engine, a radial design well in advance of its time, put out 52.4 hp for its 124-pound weight

Bottom of page
Langley's *Aerodrome* was launched twice from its houseboat catapult only to plunge each time into the Potomac River

Langley knew that steam could not give him the lightweight power he would need for this larger machine. And so he turned to the internal combustion engine, already being used widely as the power plant for the newly introduced automobile. With a bespectacled assistant named Charles M. Manly, Langley began searching for an engine which would weigh about 100 pounds and develop at least 12 horsepower. A New York manufacturer, S.M. Balzer, promised to make such an engine but was unable to deliver. Other companies both in America and Europe said it was impossible. Manly was convinced from the engines he had studied, however, that he could make what Langley wanted. Working with the original Balzer engine, Manly first produced an engine weighing 108 pounds and delivering 18.5 horsepower, then made an improved version with a weight of 124 pounds and developing a fantastic — for that time — 52.4 horsepower. Water-cooled, with five cylinders placed in radial fashion, the Manly engine was far ahead of its time. And as Langley and his devoted assistant were soon to find out, it was far ahead also of the craft it was supposed to power.

By the standards of any age Langley's 1903 *Aerodrome* was an awkward spectacle. It had monoplane wings set in tandem with one pair forward and the other aft, and with a four-vaned tail bringing up the rear. Wings were placed at a severe dihedral (angle) and were deeply cambered (curved) from leading edge to trailing edge. The only controllable element of the plane was the tail, which could be moved up and down but not horizontally. Not only was the plane unprecedented in appearance, but it was unprecedented in cost. More than $70,000 was spent on the project, including the War Department's $50,000 and an additional sum of at least $20,000 from the Smithsonian.

After some preliminary tests with his old models, Langley had the *Aerodrome* mounted aboard a specially built catapult houseboat and readied for a flight on the Potomac about 40 miles south of Washington. The weather was not too good for the first trial on Oct. 7, 1903, but both money and the patience of official sponsors were running out. Manly gave the signal for a line to be cut, and with engine resounding, the craft rushed forward. As soon as it had left the catapult it plunged straight into the river. Manly, still dripping wet, was besieged by newspaper reporters. Why had the *Aerodrome* failed, they wanted to know. The unnerved pilot could only guess it was due to the airplane's lack of balance and stability. But the next day Langley said a snag in the catapult system had caused the crash. He would rebuild it, he said, and try again. By December 8 the *Aerodrome* was ready again, and once more Manly sat at the controls with engine wide open ready to give the signal. Once

again the line was cut and this time the plane nosed almost straight up as soon as it cleared the houseboat deck, falling back with a sickening splash into the water. This time Manly barely escaped from the wreckage.

That spelled the end of Langley's experiments in aeronautics. No one knew exactly why the *Aerodrome* had failed the second time — it could have been the catapult mechanism or some structural weakness of the plane itself. It mattered little to the War Department, however, which now withdrew its support of further trials. With the nation's press hurling broadsides of sarcasm and insult at him, the sensitive and aging secretary of the Smithsonian turned away from his work in the aerial field, embittered and hurt. He died three years later.

At the very moment Langley's *Aerodrome* toppled for the last time into the Potomac, the Wright brothers were approaching their own encounter with destiny. Orville was in Dayton, where he had returned briefly to help turn out a replacement part for the Wright *Flyer*. Wilbur was waiting at their windswept campsite on the beach at Kitty Hawk, N.C., fidgeting over the craft the two had patiently assembled there. Just nine days after the Langley fiasco, on Dec. 17, 1903, Orville flew the frail biplane a distance of 120 feet — a tiny jump by present-day standards but a giant step into aerial history for the Wrights. "This flight lasted only 12 seconds," Orville later wrote, "but it was nevertheless the first in the history of the world in which a machine carrying a man had raised itself by its own power into the air in full flight, had sailed forward without reduction of speed, and had finally landed at a point as high as that from which it started."

The Wrights may have lacked formal education — neither ever received a high school diploma — but they prepared for their great aerial breakthrough as thoroughly and as scientifically in their own way as Langley had in his. The youngest of five children of a United Brethren Church bishop, they learned early in life of the importance of frugality and hard work. Together they published a weekly newspaper and took on printing jobs. In 1882, when Wilbur was 25 and Orville 21, they opened a bicycle shop where in the period of a few years they were building their own custom-made bicycles.

The Wrights' interest in flying developed during their bicycle-building days in the 1890's, when they read about Lilienthal's flights in Germany. As young boys they had tinkered with a toy, rubber-band-powered helicopter. Now, stimulated by the soaring achievements of the "father of gliding flights," they scoured libraries and wrote letters trying to find fresh material on the problem of flight. In 1899 they built their first aerial device, a biplane kite. This very first effort applied a principle of great importance to their later success — a "wing-warping" system by which they controlled the kite's balance with four strings from the ground. It worked by twisting the edges of the wings down or up against the airflow, thus dropping or lifting the wings in flight as desired.

These bachelor brothers, always neat as a pin in stiff collars and neckties, were just getting started. Now they wrote to Octave Chanute, author of one of the best flying histories of the period, and explained their experiments. That began a valuable friendship during which Chanute provided them with much assistance and encouragement. They also wrote to the United States Weather Bureau in order to find out where in this country the steadiest, strongest winds prevailed. The Bureau listed Kitty Hawk as one such site, and in an exchange of letters with the Kitty Hawk Weather Station they became convinced that it had the kind of breezes they would need to test their theories of

The success of the Wright's 1902 glider (below) paved the way for the historic powered flight on December 17, 1903

lift and control.

Arriving at the remote coastal sand strip in October 1900, Wilbur and Orville went about building a glider that included not only their wing-warping system but a movable horizontal elevator in front for additional control. At first there were a few disappointments. Winds didn't blow as hard and steady as they expected, and the wings they had constructed on the basis of Lilienthal's designs didn't provide the lift they wanted. But the number of short successful glides they made showed that at least their front elevator and wing-warping systems were working well. The problem of control seemed solveable.

The next summer, 1901, the Ohio brothers returned to the Carolina coast, this time locating their camp a few miles south of Kitty Hawk. There they assembled a bigger glider than the 1900 model. Unfortunately, it didn't live up to the promise of their earlier craft. Orville and Wilbur were baffled by its erratic behavior and lack of steadiness. In addition, much of the technical information they had obtained through researching previous flyers seemed wrong. They went home discouraged; Wilbur commented that he didn't think man would fly in a thousand years. But by September, in a speech at Chicago, he was vigorously attacking the calculations of previous experimenters. And when they returned to the bicycle shop the brothers rigged a six-foot-long wind tunnel to find out where they were going awry. Their wind tunnel tests proved tedious and difficult, but they paid off in much added knowledge.

The Wrights went back to Kitty Hawk with new confidence. Their 1902 glider was refined in many ways over their previous one, with an added tail, improved wing design with less curvature, and a wing warping change requiring the operator to move his hips on a cradle to keep lateral balance instead of using foot controls. The new craft flew beautifully except for a fresh problem caused by the new tail. About once in every 50 flights the glider went into a puzzling tailspin (the brothers called it "well-digging") and Orville decided after a sleepless night that movable rudders should be installed instead of their fixed tail. The next morning Wilbur added the suggestion that the rudder and wing warping controls should be interconnected so that the spin could be automatically corrected by manipulating only one control mechanism. With these important modifications, the 1902 glider made more than 1,000 flights from the Kitty Hawk sands. The Wrights returned to Dayton certain that the next year they would attempt powered flight with a new and even larger machine.

Although the Wrights had by now conquered such obstacles as lift and control, one major problem remained — power. Their investigations so far had shown them that in order to achieve powered flight they would need an engine producing at least eight horsepower and weighing no more than 20 pounds per horsepower. Such an engine was simply not available on the commercial market, so they decided to build their own. What they turned out that winter was "a very pleasant surprise" in Orville's words — a square engine employing four in-line, water-cooled cylinders set horizontally, producing 12 horsepower and weighing, before installation, 152 pounds. The engine turned over at slightly over 1000 revolutions per minute.

The Wrights also found an unexpected problem which they proceeded to study in their patient way and solve. This was the design of propellers, which had been in marine use for a century but which, they discovered, had never been given a set of formal specifications. After some heated arguments, Wilbur and Orville finally built a propeller far more efficient than the ones Prof. Langley and others had designed. Their plan was to mount two of them in pusher fashion behind the engine, which would drive them with a bicycle chain.

Now the Wrights faced the most critical period of their experiments. Both physically and mentally they could not have been better prepared. Both in excellent shape, Wilbur, then 36 years old, weighed about 140 pounds, and Orville, 32, was 145 pounds. Mentally they were confident and ready for the task ahead. All of their tough German-Swiss ancestral stock and all their own mechanical skill, imagination and determination would be brought into play that fall of 1903.

Troubles began to multiply soon after their arrival at Kitty Hawk. The weather started out stormy and then turned cold, delaying the assembly of their new *Flyer*. In its first mounted test, the engine backfired and badly twisted a tubular propeller shaft; the brothers sent back to Dayton for strengthened shafts. Sprockets on the new shafts kept coming loose; repairs were made with bicycle tire cement. Then one of the repaired shafts cracked and Orville rushed back to Ohio for new solid steel ones. When he returned on Dec. 11, he brought with him not only the replacement parts but the news of Langley's second failure on the Potomac.

On Dec. 14 Wilbur made an unsuccessful attempt. The *Flyer* slid along the wooden rail the Wrights had devised for launching, climbed sharply a few feet, then stalled and skittered onto the sand. Some repairs were necessary, but by the 17th Orville was ready to make his try.

A more forlorn setting could hardly be imagined for that historical occasion. It was cold on the desolate beach and winds were really too high for what the Wrights believed was a sensible attempt. But the brothers, with only four men and a boy looking on, were determined. Orville climbed aboard, positioned himself prone on the lower wing and revved the engine. Head up, he released the wire that held the machine to the track. It moved forward with Wilbur running alongside. At the end of a 40-foot run it rose into the air and moved unsteadily forward into the wind. It came back to earth 120 feet from the point where it had taken off.

The Wrights made three more flights the same day, with Wilbur's final one covering 852 feet in a time of 59 seconds. "Success four flights Thursday morning," Orville wired home to their father, "all against 21-mile wind started from level with engine power alone average speed through air 31-miles longest 59 seconds inform press home Christmas. Orville Wright."

Just as the press had trumpeted Langley's failure, it ignored the Wrights' achievement. On a tip from the telegraph operator who had sent Orville's message, one newspaper, the *Virginia-Pilot,* picked up the story and ran it — full of errors — across the top of page one. Another, the *Cincinnati Enquirer,* put a modest account on its front page. But the man who could have told the world about it, a telegraph editor and AP correspondent in Dayton named Frank Tunison, shrugged it off. If the flight had been 59 minutes instead of 59 seconds, he is reputed to have said, it would be newsworthy.

Not until the following March did the flight receive its first mention in a scientific publication, A.I. Root's *Gleanings In Bee Culture.* And not until December 1906 — three years after Kitty Hawk — did the prestigious *Scientific American* get around to acknowledging the importance of the Wrights' achievement.

By that time the word was out in the fraternity of aerial enthusiasts that the Wrights had flown and were constantly improving their machine. Soon others were in the field, most actively in France and the United States. Some of them had new ideas, while others patterned their aircraft after the brothers' designs. Their efforts added to those of the Wrights would nurture the infant airplane through a decade of undreamed advancement. However, 1903 remains as the pivotal year — the year when Man fashioned his own wings and flew for the first time.

2
The Beginnings

The Wright brothers' flight, pioneering achievement though it was, could not have been made without the attempts at flight during the centuries before them. Much as their Kitty Hawk *Flyer* was the unique product of their own determined efforts and inventive minds, the Wrights did have some guidelines to follow in the writings and practical experiments of others. As avid readers of flying history they knew what had already been accomplished, and what could not be done, as they set out to build their own aircraft. And even though they were forced to discard some of the data of their precursors, as they were in the case of glider-builder Otto Lilienthal, they drew inspiration from the work of those earlier men. Let us look back at some of those early experiments in flight and see how men groped for some means to raise themselves from the earth and soar through the skies like birds. Some of their findings pointed the way toward the Wrights; much of it came to nothing. Some of it presaged entirely different forms of flight, each with its own colorful history.

Thousands of flying devices were imagined or attempted over the millennia, but most may be placed into four categories:

1. Ornithopters, or wing-flapping craft.
2. Helicopters, or craft capable of rising vertically through use of rotating wings.
3. Lighter-than-air craft, which include both balloons and dirigibles.
4. Fixed-wing aircraft including gliders and power-driven airplanes.

Of all the flying concepts, "wing-flapping" is probably the oldest. It goes back to the earliest yearnings of Man to imitate birds, and crops up repeatedly in the myths and legends of antiquity. The most famous of these concerns Daedalus and Icarus and how the latter lost his wings of wax and feathers by flying too close to the sun, but it is only one of many such stories. Eventually, at-tempts to turn these fantasies into reality were made by men who hitched wing-like contrivances to their bodies and jumped off medieval towers or the ramparts of city walls. The consequences for these eccentric "tower jumpers" were predictably disastrous. Yet, a number of learned men earnestly believed that the true path to flight was in direct imitation of birds. Among these believers were the early English scientist Roger Bacon (1214-92) and the Italian genius Leonardo da Vinci (1452-1519). Leonardo's interest in flight led him to draw prophetic designs for a parachute and helicopter, but he reserved his greatest enthusiasm for wing-flapping. He sketched both prone-type and standing ornithopters, supposing that the flapping power could be provided by human muscles. After Leonardo's death, it was shown both in real-life attempts and in a book by the Italian scholar Borelli that the muscles of men were not up to the job of beating wings, and enthusiasm cooled for further experiments on bird-like ornithopters.

Artist da Vinci was intrigued with the idea of flight

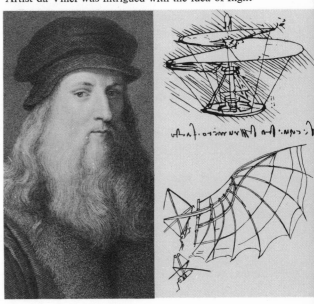

Balloonist Jean Blanchard
made the first free flight
in America in 1794

as participants.

The helicopter, like the ornithopter, had its origins in antiquity. As early as the 4th century B.C., the Chinese amused themselves with "flying tops" which mounted bird feathers in propeller fashion atop a spinning stick. It is doubtful that anyone could have recognized the potential of this plaything at the time, however, for a working helicopter needed power then undreamed of to lift and sustain it aloft. Later, the great Da Vinci saw its possibilities in rough designs which incorporated Archimedes' principle of the rotating screw as a rotor blade. And in 1783, when Launoy and Bienvenu demonstrated a Chinese flying top before the French Academy of Sciences, the imaginations of European scientists were fired with new visions of vertical flight.

Interest in the wing-flappers was revived briefly in the 19th century when a number of attempts were made to give them a mechanical source of power. Models by the Frenchmen Jobert and Pénaud made meager flights using the power of twisted rubber bands. Trouve of France used blank cartridges firing into a tube to flap the wings of his model, and the Australian Hargrave employed rubber bands, compressed air and even clockwork to propel his hybrid fixed-wing and ornithopter models.

The best-known American to be attracted to wing-flapping was John P. Holland, who was already famous as a builder of submarines when, in 1907, he published the views he had formed from experiments made nearly 50 years earlier. Holland declared that an operator could attach two transverse wing arms to his body and treadle himself through the air, and predicted that a "new order of existence" would stem from such contraptions. His "new order" would surely come as aviation boomed in the 20th century, but the wing-flappers would not be included

Several interesting approaches were made to the helicopter idea during the 19th century. One was by Sir George Cayley in England who found a solution for the problem of torque, or twist, in a rapidly turning rotor by designing two sets of blades turning in opposite directions. A few years later the famed American inventor Thomas A. Edison tinkered with a model vertical craft but gave up his work on it after concluding that he needed a much more powerful engine than was available in the 1880's.

Not long after the Wrights flew, two French inventors produced primitive helicopters which gave better promise of things to come than actual performance. Louis Breguet took his four-rotor craft to a height of about two feet in 1907 for a period of one minute. Later the same year Paul Cornu whirled six feet off the ground for only a third of a minute. Both used infant versions of the internal combustion engine, the power plant of aviation's future.

America entered the helicopter picture in 1909 when Emile Berliner and J. Newton

Baldwin (photo left) made America's first parachute jump at San Francisco in 1887

Flight trial of Capt. Thomas Baldwin's balloon dirigible at Fort Myer, 1908

Williams got a two-rotor machine to rise a few feet off the ground. Berliner, a reputable scientist who had invented the gramophone, decided this arrangement was too dangerous to develop further, although he and his son Henry built improved machines which they marketed during the 1920's.

Frustrations were also encountered by a young Russian, Igor Sikorsky, but he overcame early setbacks to become one of the most respected names in the field of helicopters. In 1909 Sikorsky constructed a 25-horsepower helicopter in his native Kiev after examining Cornu's machine in France. The first Sikorsky shook so much it nearly flew apart, but the following year the inventor produced a lighter, sturdier model which rose a few feet off the ground — so long as no one was aboard. Sikorsky then dropped work on helicopters to concentrate on airplanes. Thirty years later, by then a prominent airplane manufacturer in America, Sikorsky returned to experiments in vertical flight and built the first practical helicopter in the United States. In so doing he fathered a whole new branch of the aviation industry.

No spinning rotors or flapping wings were necessary to send lighter-than-air balloons soaring skyward. They rose chemically, not mechanically, and with a graceful ease that awed the populace of Europe and America after their introduction in France in 1783. But appearances are often deceptive; balloons and the powered dirigibles which derived from them carried the seeds of their own destruction in their pleasing lines. Balloons in free flight were at the mercy of air currents and winds and thus lacked the control essential to true flight (this was a condition which plagued even dirigibles driven by powerful engines). Most lighter-than-air ships also used hydrogen, a gas so highly inflammable that it could turn its carrier into an inferno in an instant. By the time a nonflammable substitute was found in helium, dirigibles were being abandoned in favor of airplanes which were safer.

Within a few years after the Montgolfier brothers lofted their first balloon in France, all of Europe and America were agog over these gaudy gas bags which defied gravity. Although the first American ascension is reputed to have been made by a 13-year-old boy in 1784, the first real balloon trip in the United States was made 10 years later by a Frenchman, Jean Pierre Blanchard, from Philadelphia to Deptford Township in New Jersey. Ballooning became a favorite spectator sport. Crowds thrilled to exhibitions at carnivals and fairs; a throng of 20,000 watched Charles F. Durant make the first ascent from New York City in 1830.

17

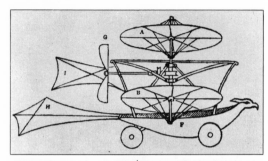

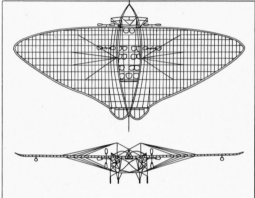

A more ambitious role for ballooning was envisioned by John Wise, a barnstorming "aeronaut" who believed a balloon could cross the Atlantic Ocean by riding west-to-east air currents. In 1859 he and three companions embarked on a trial run from St. Louis to the Eastern Seaboard where they planned to prepare for the actual ocean crossing. They fell short of their destination when a storm forced them down near the shores of Lake Ontario after a harrowing trip of more than 800 miles. Wise proposed another transatlantic attempt a few years later but the venture failed. The intrepid balloonist continued flying well into his old age and finally disappeared while he was making a trip over Lake Michigan.

Balloons stirred new interest as weapons of war when they were used by the Union forces during the Civil War under the direction of Thaddeus S.C. Lowe. Although not the first to make battle observations from the sky (the French Army had used balloons in 1784), Lowe both impressed President Lincoln with his demonstrations of their effectiveness and gave substantial help in several battles with his sightings of positions held by Confederate armies.

Dirigibles evolved from balloons as power was added and an elongated shape was adopted to reduce air resistance. Henri Giffard of France flew the first powered dirigible in 1852 using a low-powered steam engine (3-horsepower). Not until after the turn of the century, however, did dirigibles regularly install gasoline engines. In France, the wealthy Alberto Santos-Dumont thrilled Parisians with his frequent flights over the city, and in America a carnival parachute jumper, Thomas S. Baldwin, built the first successful dirigible in the nation with the aid of a young motorcycle manufacturer, Glenn H. Curtiss. Baldwin sold a later airship to the U.S. Army in 1908, and it was still under-

going trials at Fort Myer when Orville Wright arrived to begin tests of the Wright biplane.

A seesaw chronicle of fame and ill-fortune marked the following years of dirigible activity. Refined in design and driven by improved engines, the glistening giants of the sky made many valuable exploratory flights as well as opening what seemed to be a comfortable new mode of commercial travel. But one after another of the great dirigibles met a disastrous end. One early failure came in 1910 when journalist Walter Wellman tried to cross the Atlantic in his airship *America* but, with his crew, had to abandon ship after drifting helplessly for over a thousand miles. After World War I a series of dirigible accidents shocked the world, until the explosion of the German *Hindenburg* in 1937 put an end to their story.

Fixed-wing aircraft did not come first in the long history of flying, but ultimately they worked the best and led to the development of the modern airplane. Intensive work on the theory and behavior of fixed-wing aircraft begins with Sir George Cayley, an En-

glish baronet who, during his long lifetime, dealt with an amazing array of problems connected with flight. Not only did Cayley set forth the basic principles of heavier-than-air flight, but his aerodynamic research afforded a new understanding of the whole mystery of flight. He even proposed a light wheel for airplane undercarriages and suggested internal combustion engines and jet propulsion. Not the least of his contributions was a full-size glider built in 1852 or 1853 which, he wrote, could "sail majestically from the top of a hill to any given point of the plain below it with perfect steadiness and safety." For his many discoveries in the field of flying Cayley is aptly called "The Father of Aerial Navigation."

New advances were made in fixed-wing airplanes during the 19th century by William Henson, John Stringfellow and Horatio Phillips in England and by Jean-Marie le Bris, Félix du Temple and Alphonse Pénaud in France. Around 1890 Sir Hiram Maxim, already famed for the Maxim machinegun built a strange three-ton, multi-wing craft that almost took off through sheer uncontrollable power.

Toward the close of the century, in 1893, the German Otto Lilienthal started his experiments with gliders which were to have a profound effect on aerial progress. Convinced that actual flying experience was the best teacher, Lilienthal built numerous bird-like gliders in which he soared off hills or huge man-made mounds. In Scotland, Percy Pilcher constructed several promising gliders, and was working toward powered flight when a crash ended his career. In America, the engineer and aerial enthusiast Octave Chanute built single and multi-wing gliders and flew them from the shores of Lake Michigan. The work of these glider-builders soon led to the Wrights' own labors on gliders at Kitty Hawk and then on to the construction of their first powered airplane.

19

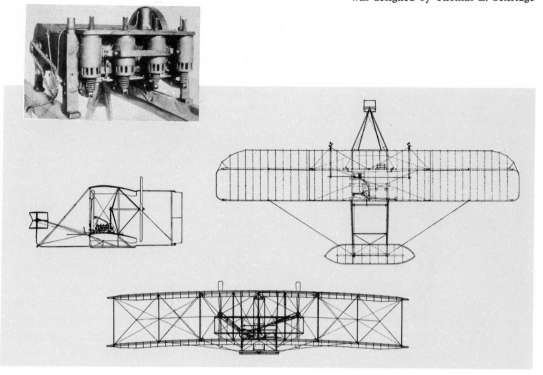

The Wright *Flyer* of 1903 and the Wright engine. The combination of lifting surfaces, controls and power that made possible human flight

Opposite
Red Wing, the first airplane of the Aerial Experimental Association, was designed by Thomas E. Selfridge

Gliders gave to flight the progress it needed in design and control, but automobiles gave it the development of power. Almost as much as the airplane, the "horseless carriage" needed a light, reliable and powerful engine to drive it. And when automobile manufacturers strove constantly to build a better gasoline internal combustion engine, they were making what the airplane needed, too. Certainly the airplane engine had to be even lighter than its automobile counterpart, but that could be engineered by early airmen like Manly and the Wrights, most of whom had a knowledge of auto mechanics.

Until the arrival of the gasoline engine, experimenters tried every method of power they could lay their hands on, from rubber bands to electricity to compressed air. Steam was sometimes used — as in Ader's bat-winged machines, Maxim's big biplane and Langley's early aerodrome models — but the steam engine's great weight in proportion to the power it produced made it apparent that it could not be used to propel into the air the fragile gliders of that day.

Internal combustion engines made their aerial debut in dirigibles. Paul Haenlein drove his airship in Germany with a Lenoir-type engine in 1872, using coal gas for fuel. In 1879 a Daimler-made, benzine-burning engine powered another German airship which was wrecked, however, before it could fly. Later dirigibles could use the vastly improved automobile engines of the turn-of-the-century period with only minor changes. The world's first practical dirigible built by the Lebaudy brothers in France in 1902 had a 40-horsepower Daimler which was virtually a large edition of the Daimler car engine.

It remained for the Wrights to devise an engine which would meet the even greater weight requirements of heavier-than-air flight, and combine it with a workable aircraft. Now the long years of tentative experiments, of searching in the dark for the answers to the mysteries of flight, were at last ending. Now was to begin a new age of development and determination, of hard work and heartaches which would change the course of the history of the whole world.

3
The Challengers

On an icy afternoon early in 1908, Glenn H. Curtiss, a serious young man known primarily as a manufacturer of motorcycles, bent to the task of adjusting eight separate carburetors on a flying machine resting on a frozen lake in upstate New York. Curtiss listened closely as the engine idled, adjusting one carburetor, then another. Seemingly satisfied, he straightened up and jumped off. One of the small group gathered around the craft raised his arm and, after a few tense seconds, lowered it. There was a growing roar from the engine, and the frail machine slid over the ice until it became airborne. The watching men let out a whoop and then fell silent as the plane beat its way into the gray sky. Moments later, still plainly in view, the little craft settled back to the ice and the men ran toward it. Jubilant, they pounded the pilot on the back. Then they remembered the business at hand and unfurled a measuring tape. They made it 318 feet and 11 inches. Not a bad distance, they congratulated themselves, for a fledgling effort in the new science of aeronautics.

The date was March 12, 1908, and the place, Keuka Lake, New York. The plane was *Red Wing,* named after the bright red silk that covered her biplane wings. There was cause for celebration, for this was the first successful powered flight made by a newly formed group called the Aerial Experiment Association. *Red Wing* would become the first of four biplanes built by the A.E.A. within the coming year. The short hop it made that cold, overcast Sunday — never more than eight feet above the ice — marked the first real challenge to the aerial supremacy of the Wright brothers on the American continent. It also would mark the emergence of a new leader in American aviation, Glenn Hammond Curtiss.

In some ways, the story of Curtiss' rise parallels that of the Wrights. Like the Ohio brothers he came from a family of modest means, and as a youngster he liked tinkering with mechanical things. While still in his teens he worked up a trade in bicycles and bike repairing. But unlike the Wrights, who were fascinated by problems of aerodynamics,

The Aerial Experiment Association organized in 1907 (from left) "Casey" Baldwin, Lt. Selfridge, Curtiss, Dr. Bell, John McCurdy and visitor, Augustus Post of the Aero Club of America

The Aerial Experiment Association organized in 1907 (from left) "Casey" Baldwin, Lt. Selfridge, Curtiss, Dr. Bell, John McCurdy and visitor, Augustus Post of the Aero Club of America

the lean, strong fellow from Hammondsport, N.Y., was drawn to engines. He built his first in 1900 using a small tomato can for a carburetor. At first he installed his primitive engines on bicycles, but by 1903 he had started his own company for manufacturing motorcycles. He not only built them, he raced them well enough to give him local fame as a daredevil on wheels. His reputation spread nationally in the spring of 1906 when he cracked the world speed record by driving a custom-built motorcycle an astonishing 136.47 miles an hour over the sands of Ormond Beach, Florida. It established a record that stood on the ground until 1911 and in the air until nearly the end of World War I.

Curtiss' reputation as an engine builder soon landed him in aviation. A veteran California balloonist and self-styled aerial "captain," Thomas S. Baldwin, persuaded the young manufacturer to adapt one of his two-cylinder motorcycle engines to propel a dirigible he was building. The transfer worked. On Aug. 4, 1904, Baldwin made a short and slightly unsteady flight in the new *California Arrow* from Oakland, Calif., with the air-cooled Curtiss providing power. For a while Curtiss mixed motorcycle-making with the further development of *California Arrow*. It was in this airship that the Hammondsporter himself flew for the first time. He told Baldwin afterward that he had enjoyed the experience — except that the *Arrow* went too slowly to suit his taste.

One day in 1906, inventor Alexander Graham Bell paused before the display of a new V-8 engine at a New York Aero Show. Impressed, the distinguished scientist struck up a conversation with the young man behind the booth. He was the engine's manufacturer, Glenn Curtiss, and soon Bell was saying they must get together for a long talk. Although Bell's greatest achievement was the invention of the telephone, he had long been interested in aviation. He had been a champion of Langley's experiments and a witness to the 1903 disaster of the *Aerodrome* on the Potomac. Then nearly 60, Bell was working on his own dream of flight: a tetrahedral kite whose main feature was a screen-like surface composed of more than 1,000 four-sided, triangular-plane cells. Searching for reliable power for the kite, he suddenly saw Curtiss as the man who could provide it. After a new discussion, it was agreed that Curtiss would build two lightweight four-cylinder engines. The first was delivered in 1907 but did not perform as expected. The expert hand of the manufacturer clearly was needed, and so Bell asked Curtiss to join him — with a handsome money offer as an inducement.

Gathered that summer at Bell's rambling house on Lake Bras d'Or in Baddeck, Nova Scotia, besides Curtiss were two young Canadian engineers, John A.D. McCurdy and Frederick W. (Casey) Baldwin (no relation to Capt. Baldwin), and a young U.S. Army lieutenant, Thomas E. Selfridge, who was detached from duty with the new Aeronautical Division of the Signal Corps to study flying with Bell. The men hit it off immediately. Talking late into the night in the quiet comfort of Bell's home, they agreed to form the Aerial Experiment Association, a loose arrangement under which each would

help the other in advancing his own aviation ideas. Except for their mutual recognition of Bell as leader, they would all pull together to "get into the air," as their charter said.

The first order of business was the completion of a new tetrahedral kite to be known as *Cygnet*. Larger than any previous device Bell had built (it had 3,000 cells), *Cygnet* never had a chance to show it could fly with its Curtiss engine. On a test glide it went down in the lake and was severely damaged while being towed to recovery.

Although *Cygnet's* disablement was a bitter disappointment to Bell, he quickly agreed that the A.E.A. should proceed with the more conventional ideas of its members. Transferring their operations to Hammondsport to be closer to the facilities of Curtiss' factory, the A.E.A. turned out the first of their biplanes, *Red Wing*. Despite the hopes it encouraged by its short flight off Keuka Lake, *Red Wing's* career was brief. On its second flight a few days later the little airplane, designed by Selfridge and powered by a 25-horsepower engine, landed hard on the ice. "Casey" Baldwin, at the controls, was only slightly injured but the plane was crippled beyond reasonable repair.

White Wing — so named because white muslin covered its wings — became the second A.E.A. creation, built according to Baldwin's blueprints. In place of runners carried by *Red Wing* three landing wheels were installed, and controls in the form of crude ailerons were added where its predecessor had none. *White Wing* made four successful flights that included one of 1,017 feet, but it had to be scrapped after a fifth ended in a crash with McCurdy aboard.

June Bug was the third and most promising aircraft yet built by the A.E.A. It was similar to earlier designs in that it carried distinctive "concavo-convex" wings — wings that bowed toward each other near the tips in an effort to

provide stability. But it had an important variation in that it had improved ailerons that reduced both the drag of *White Wing* and that plane's bothersome tendency to turn while in level flight. It proved a winner in a widely publicized distance trophy event held at Stony Brook Farm Racetrack in Hammondsport sponsored by *Scientific American* magazine. Taking off in a cloud of smoke with Curtiss aboard, *June Bug* traveled well beyond the required distance of one kilometer by covering 5,090 feet in one minute and 42 1/5 seconds. This was later hailed as the first "public flight" in America — an injustice to the Wrights who by 1908 had flown many times in full view of the public.

A controversy now arose over the A.E.A.'s ailerons which dogged Curtiss throughout his airplane-making years. The Wright brothers brought suit, claiming they were stolen from their patented wing-warping system. The Ohio brothers were upheld in court, but it was the aileron concept which was sustained by history. Ailerons became the basic lateral control feature of future airplanes. (It should be noted that it was neither the Wrights nor Curtiss who finally was recognized as the inventor of ailerons. That honor went to Dr. William W. Christmas of Washington, D.C., who flew a plane of his own design a few days before the *Red Wing* flight, and who was awarded a patent for his aileron system by the U.S. Government.)

On Sept. 17, 1908, the A.E.A. received a blow that disrupted its progress and eventually spelled its end. Lt. Selfridge had been recalled to Washington to witness Army tests of the new Wright biplane at Fort Myer, Va. Orville began the trials early in September, impressing the military observers on solo and passenger flights. The 17th was scheduled for the final test, and Selfridge, a little nervous, settled himself into the seat alongside Orville. The Wright *Flyer* catapulted off its launching

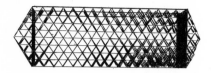

track, rose into the air and circled the field three times. On the fourth circle a crowd of about 2,000 saw a puff of smoke. Aboard the plane, Orville said later, there was a tapping sound and then two thumps. The plane nosed down, vibrating violently, and crashed in a cloud of dust. Orville spent seven weeks in the hospital recovering from hip, leg and rib fractures. Selfridge, muttering, "Take this damn thing off my back," was hauled from the wreckage and died a few hours later. A crack in the propeller, newly installed for the final test, was determined as the cause of the accident. The mishap cut short a career of great promise for the 26-year-old lieutenant.

The stunned A.E.A. decided to push ahead with its experiments. Bell built a new and even larger *Cygnet* but it never became successfully airborne. A fourth airplane, *Silver Dart,* was designed and flown mostly by McCurdy; it logged 1,000 miles over many flights, and became the first airplane to fly in Canada. Curtiss began a project of his own by fitting the old *June Bug* with two pontoons and rechristening her *Loon.* Feeble though this effort proved to be (*Loon* refused to become unglued from the waters of Keuka Lake), it represented the first of Curtiss' many contributions toward the development of naval aviation.

Demoralized by Selfridge's death and lacking money for new projects, the A.E.A. was dissolved by mutual agreement. Members went their separate ways. Bell's further work with tetrahedral kites proved an aviation dead end. "Casey" Baldwin soon gave up active flying. McCurdy gained headlines in the next few years as a stunt flyer, and made an overwater hop from Florida to Cuba, ditching in sight of the Cuban coast. But he too eventually gave up flying actively. Curtiss alone went on to make an imprint in American and world aviation.

In the meantime, the Wrights were busier than ever. By March 1909 — when the A.E.A. was breaking up — Wilbur was in France winding up a triumphal series of exhibitions before the awed greats of European aviation. Soon he would be joined by Orville, who had recovered from the Fort Myer crash, for a series of new demonstrations in Italy.

Behind the brothers lay years of labor that finally had given them recognition as the leaders of international aviation. After their history-making flight at Kitty Hawk in 1903, the Wrights had moved their operations to a cow pasture outside Dayton. There they flew a slightly more powerful *Flyer* about 100 times. But many of those 1904 flights caused disappointment, either because they didn't reach the Kitty Hawk distance record, or because of a persistent problem with the plane's lateral control.

With their 1905 machine, however, the Wrights made a comeback. This was dubbed *Flyer III* and, although it employed the 1904 engine, it had improved wing design and controls. Several long distances were achieved that year, but they passed unnoticed by all except a few. This was despite the fact that a trolley line passed near Huffman pasture in plain view of the brothers' experiments. The Wrights later became secretive about their work, but in those days they welcomed witnesses. Once that year they invited a contingent of newspapermen, but as fate would have it engine trouble prevented them from getting off the ground that day.

The Wrights were first-rate scientists but they were hard-headed businessmen too. After their 1905 season they called a halt to further flights in order to concentrate on the sale of their product. First they turned to the U.S. Government in the belief that it would be interested in *Flyer III* for reconnaissance purposes. Twice they offered it to the War

Department and were refused each time. Their second offer made clear they would provide a finished product without government financial aid — "practical flying-machines suitable for scouting purposes," they wrote. Incredibly, the government replied that it wasn't interested "until a machine is produced which by actual operation is shown to be able to produce horizontal flight and carry an operator."

Just 19 days earlier, on Oct. 5, 1905, the Wrights had set a world's distance record of 24 miles.

Now the brothers turned to British and French interests, both of which had made personal contact with them. But negotiations fell through. Then late in 1907, spurred by the personal interest of President Theodore Roosevelt, the War Department called for bids on a military airplane it specified was to fly nonstop for "about one hour" at a speed of 40 miles an hour. Forty-one bids were submitted but only three met specifications. And of these only the Wrights' bid — at $25,000 with delivery in 200 days — turned out to be substantial. The government accepted it on Feb. 8, 1908, and Wilbur and Orville once again journeyed to their old haunt at Kitty Hawk to regain their flying skill (neither had flown since the end of the '05 season). By late spring they left North Carolina with their expert flying touch and a plan of action. Orville would demonstrate the *Flyer* for the U.S. Army, while Wilbur would go to France at the invitation of a syndicate forming to manufacture Wright planes.

Now came the Wrights' finest hour. Wilbur, sober-faced and calm in his tie, starched collar and workingman's cap, won the hearts of the French with flights of 12 miles and more at Le Mans. Orville's tests at Fort Myer included at least four hops of over an hour's duration. And although these ended in tragedy, they clearly impressed the Army

brass. Said Major George O. Squier who had been Orville's second passenger: "Of course we deplore the accident, but no one who saw the flights . . . could doubt for an instant that the problem of aerial navigation was solved."

If the Wrights hadn't exactly conquered the problem of flight, they understood the solutions to it. Early they had realized that no aircraft could be built, with the materials and data then available, that could fly itself. French designers and flyers believed inherent stability must be built into an airplane so it could be "chauffeured" through the air, a concept that delayed the development of aviation in Europe. The Wrights knew they had to have extraordinary ability to manage heavier-than-air flights, and set out to acquire it. Just as important, the brothers knew their airplane must have good mechanical controls that would respond to a pilot's touch. By 1908 they had perfected their wing-warping system as far as it would go. The combination of controls and human skill worked wonders. Orville literally ran rings around the Fort Myer parade ground, circling it 57 times one day in as many minutes. Wilbur held aviators and the press spellbound with his delicate maneuvering at Le Mans.

One innovation in the 1908 model was the pilot-passenger arrangement. Instead of the neck-wrenching, prone position dictated by their earlier planes, it placed pilot and rider in a seated position. The '08 *Flyer* also had an improved engine employing vertical instead of the previously favored horizontal cylinders and producing about 35 horsepower. It used the Wrights' derrick catapult for takeoff, a weight-and-pulley rig invented in 1904 to get them into the air faster.

The 1908 *Flyer* was carried over into the next year's Wright Model A, which after new tests became the Army's first airplane. Repaired and much traveled, it remained the

Curtiss, the lone American in the field, shunned altitude and distance contests to concentrate on speed events. The grand prize was the Gordon Bennett trophy, which Curtiss won doing an average 47 miles an hour over 20 kilometers. His victory, witnessed by a stupendous Saturday crowd estimated at 100,000, was an especially sweet one in that he bested Blériot and the Frenchman's vaunted monoplane by over five seconds.

Curtiss' Rheims machine, sometimes called *Golden Flyer,* was a souped-up version of the earlier *Gold Bug,* housing a V-8, water-cooled engine that delivered 50 horsepower. It used the Wright concept of an elevator forward and rudder aft (as did all the A.E.A.'s planes), but it was equipped with interplane ailerons set between the wings and had three landing wheels.

Army's only airplane until 1911 when "Aeroplane No. 2" was purchased. Ironically, this biplane, a pusher-type like the Wright plane, was built by the Wright brothers' chief rival — Glenn Curtiss.

By now Curtiss had himself become a major name in aviation. Forming a new company with Augustus M. Herring, a former Wright assistant, he built a new airplane, *Gold Bug,* which won the second *Scientific American* trophy on July 17, 1909, in New York City. A month later the stern-faced upstate New Yorker rushed to France to participate in a much-ballyhooed aviation meet outside Rheims.

The greats of European aviation gathered for the Rheims meet. Among the participating pilots were Louis Blériot, who had made the first English Channel crossing by air; the suave sportsman Hubert Latham, flying a graceful Antoinette monoplane; the daring Eugene Lefebvre, piloting a Wright biplane; and the French national air hero Henri Farman, who had entered a biplane of his and his brothers' manufacture.

The following year, Curtiss flew a similar plane from Albany to New York, winning a $10,000 prize offered by the *New York World,* plus permanent possession of the *Scientific American* trophy. A special train raced below Curtiss during the 142-mile flight down the Hudson River. In New York City thousands swarmed in streets, parks and on rooftops to see the climax. For once it was an aerial feat for all New York to see; neither his previous *Scientific American* wins nor his Rheims victory had made such an impact. The flight established Curtiss as an American air hero as well as airplane designer.

Ahead of Curtiss lay new triumphs. Out of his work in marine aviation grew the U.S. Navy Air Wing. He figured importantly, too, in the early years of Army aviation by manufacturing the famous "Jenny" biplanes that trained thousands of U.S. flyers. He also played a part in the next chapter of American aviation — the era of stunting, aerial exhibitions and international races that bemused a thrill-seeking populace before it was enveloped by World War I.

4
The Daredevils

The public had read about those daring young men in their flying machines, and suddenly they could see them in a whole series of races and competitions, fairs and exhibitions which blossomed in the carefree years before World War I. The international aviation meet at Rheims, France, was the first of the great exhibitions, drawing a crowd of an estimated quarter million to see such aerial pioneers as Glenn Curtiss, Louis Blériot, Leon Delagrange, and Henri Farman put their frail machines through their paces. Rheims was the lone notable aviation competition in 1909 but the following year numerous competitions burst forth in America and Europe. Nineteen-ten also saw the formation of several traveling aerial troupes that held audiences spellbound with their assortment of stunts.

All too often the lure of the early aerial sideshows was the possibility of an accident — the chance that blood would be spilled in a new and bizarre way. Sometimes, spectators staring into the sky got what they came for. When the Rheims meet was held there had been only four heavier-than-air fatalities, including three gliding deaths and that of Lt. Selfridge in a powered aircraft. But the death toll quickly mounted. By July 1, 1912, 155 men and three women had been killed in airplane accidents.

Rheims itself had its share of chilling spills, although none resulted in deaths. The Frenchman Henry Fournier, racing in a speed event, was caught by a gust of wind which forced his Voisin biplane to the ground in front of horrified spectators. Fournier got up, mounted a gendarme's horse and rode back to his hangar. Another French flyer, Henri Rougier, plunked his Voisin into the crowd, miraculously injuring no one. Blériot himself, the master of an English Channel crossing the previous month, had two crack-ups (Blériot reputedly had more than 50 crashes during his flying days), the second of which occurred on the last day of the competition. His airplane, an improved version of his Channel crosser, burst into flames during the final speed race but the dauntless Frenchman exited from his cockpit with nothing more than a badly burned hand.

America, not to be outdone by the smashing success of the Rheims meet, staged three big competitions the next year. Held in Los Angeles, Boston, and at Belmont Park in Long Island, N.Y., they again drew international rosters of aviators, large and celebrity-studded audiences and the usual number of thrills and spills.

Stunt flyer, Lincoln Beachey, at Niagara Falls

"America's First Aviation Meet," held in Los Angeles from Jan. 10 to 20, 1910, turned into a contest between two nations when entries boiled down to flyers from France and the United States. Louis Paulhan, star of the French team, won the altitude prize by taking his Farman biplane to 4,165 feet, a new world's record. Curtiss headed the American team comprising Clifford B. Harmon, Charles K. Hamilton, Charles F. Willard and Frank Johnson. He remained

27

on the victory trail he had established at Rheims by winning the quick-starting contest (off the ground in six and two-fifths seconds) and the speed-with-passenger record (clocking 55 miles an hour).

In September the Harvard Aeronautical Society held an international meet at Squantum on Boston Harbor which attracted the cream of society and offered $100,000 in prizes for the winning pilots. Curtiss again was on the scene with his own flying teams, as were members of the recently formed exhibition team under contract to the Wright brothers. A Curtiss performer, Ralph Johnstone, captured the duration record by flying three hours, five minutes and 40 seconds. And a Wright protégé, Walter Brookins, set a new altitude record of 4,732 feet. Boston's most sensational event, however, was a race around Boston Light which was won by one of the international greats of early aviation, Claude Grahame-White of England. Flying a Blériot monoplane, he made the overwater trip of 33 miles in 34 minutes, 1 1/5 seconds, for which he was awarded the *Boston Globe's*

$10,000 prize. Curtiss, although he flew with distinction at this meet, found himself second best in his favorite speed event: Grahame-White beat him with a time of six minutes over the five and a quarter mile course.

Interest was high for the final meet of the year at Belmont Park, L.I., held from Oct. 22 to 31. Besides the second annual presentation of the Gordon Bennett contest it featured a race from the Park to the Statue of Liberty and back, with a $10,000 prize as incentive for the winner. Again the colorful Grahame-White was the victor. He won both of the featured events — though not before several hair-raising crackups had marred one event and a wrangle among officials delayed the prize-giving in the other.

The Gordon Bennett, held on a sparkling clear Saturday morning, had two favorites in Grahame-White with a 14-cylinder, 100-horsepower Blériot, and Walter Brookins at the controls of a new Wright "Baby" racer that was supposed to have tested at over 80 miles an hour. But Brookins was out of the running almost before he started when he

The 1910 Belmont Park air meet featured the most distinguished airmen of the time — the winner in a Blériot monoplane was Grahame-White (photo right)

crashed into the turf and somersaulted the powerful new plane in front of the grandstand. Thrown clear, he picked himself up and walked away. Another contestant, sportsman Hubert Latham, spun his 100-horsepower Antoinette into a horse paddock and like Brookins emerged from the wreckage on foot. A third crash involved the Frenchman Alfred Le Blanc, who was making better time than Grahame-White over the 62.1 mile course when he ran out of gas and slammed into a telephone pole on the last lap. His plane was completely wrecked but Le Blanc lived to fly again: he suffered nothing much more than bad cuts of the face.

The 1910 Gordon Bennett race was followed by several years of official dispute. The wealthy Chicagoan John B. Moisant made the best time in a hastily purchased Blériot, but he had begun his flight past the 4 p.m. deadline under rules of the event. The Frenchman Comte de Lesseps also had support as the winner, for although he was beaten by Grahame-White, it was claimed that the Englishman had clipped the "initial pylon" — the statue itself — and thus should be disqualified. It was several years before an international committee declared Grahame-White the winner, awarding him $10,000 plus $600 interest. Grahame-White had a profitable year in America even though he didn't pocket the Statue of Liberty prize immediately. *Scientific American* magazine reported that he had made $100,000 in American flying meets.

Chicago recorded a moment of early aviation history in August 1911 with a meet sponsored by the Aero Club of Illinois. It included such star exhibition flyers as Lincoln Beachey, Eugene B. Ely, Frank Coffyn, Phil O. Parmalee, J.C. Mars, Earle R. Ovington, Hugh Robinson and Brookins, as well as an aviator who in a few years would become even more famous as an airplane builder,

T.O.M. ("Tom") Sopwith of Great Britain. Beachey dominated the speed events by taking five firsts, two seconds and three third place awards in addition to setting a new altitude record of 11,642 feet. Sopwith took home $10,000 by winning several "daily duration" contests and other events. A relative unknown, Calbraith P. Rodgers, won the total duration contest by staying aloft — in daily installments — 27 hours and 16 seconds. Rodgers, as we shall soon see, later hit headlines as the first airman to cross the American continent.

Two fatalities marred the Chicago meet, one involving young St. Croix Johnstone who dove his Moisant monoplane into Lake Michigan, and the other killing William R. Badger, who died attempting a Beachey stunt that required dipping into a hollow in Grant Park. Badger's biplane collapsed under the strain and sent its pilot to his death.

Much of the aviation action during 1911 took place in Europe, where grueling cross-country races gripped the interest of a fascinated world. But the United States had a moment of pride when the third annual Gordon Bennett speed race held in England was won by the only American entered, Charles T. Weymann. The little airman, who looked more like a banker than a flyer in his natty suits and pince-nez glasses, roared around the 94-mile course at Eastchurch in his 14-cylinder Nieuport at 78.77 miles an hour, beating the Englishman Alec Ogilvie and Frenchmen Nieuport and Le Blanc.

As interest in aviation mounted, promoters and businessmen dreamed up a variety of aerial spectacles they hoped would catch the public's fancy. Newspaper publishers often held out handsome rewards to flyers who would make some new record, such as the first New York to Philadelphia trip for which the *New York Times* and *Philadelphia Ledger* were prepared to pay $10,000. Charles

29

The first transcontinental flight — a test of endurance for man and plane. Cal Rodgers did it in a Wright "Baby" racer but it took 69 stops and 49 days

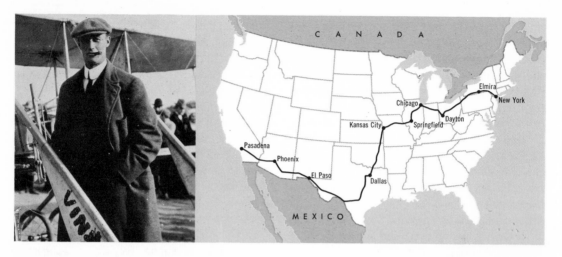

K. Hamilton, a member of the Curtiss exhibition team, won the money in June 1910 by making the trip — and back — in three hours and 27 minutes. He made the flight in a Curtiss biplane.

Another newspaper, the *Baltimore Sun,* put up $5,000 in 1910 for the first airman willing to risk his neck flying over the city. Stretches of water and open country had been managed before, but no one had purposely set out to cross the center of a large city because it was believed the air above was too turbulent. Hubert Latham, the cool, cigarette-smoking aviator who had failed in two attempts to fly the English Channel, took up the *Sun* offer and succeeded, guiding his Antoinette 2,500 feet above a watching populace estimated at more than 500,000.

Much more was at stake the following year when publisher William Randolph Hearst offered $50,000 for the first coast-to-coast flight. Cal Rodgers, his pockets still lined with the money he had won in the Chicago air meet, made the trip in a grinding course that included 69 stops and 19 crashes. And although he endured phenomenal hardship, the flight was 19 days too long to qualify for the money. Rodgers' *Vin Fiz,* a Wright "Baby" racer named after the soft

drink manufactured by the airman's sponsors, was practically another airplane when it wound up in Pasadena, Calif., so many parts had been replaced.

Fame rather than a quick fortune was the objective of a 27-year-old aviator named Harry N. Atwood when, in 1911, he determined to make what the newspapers called "the greatest cross-country flight in the history of American aviation" — Boston to Washington. The nation's capital was an early center of aviation. The Wright airplane tests had taken place in Ft. Myer across the Potomac, and in 1910 the much-headlined Grahame-White landed a Farman biplane on the street between the White House and the old War and Navy Building in order, he told reporters, to pay a return visit to President Taft who had seen the Englishman fly in the Boston meet. But nothing generated the excitement of the capital as the Atwood trip did. Washingtonians followed his progress step by step from his takeoff June 30 in Boston, to a stop in New London, Conn., to another stop in New York City where he was delayed several days. When he was ready to go again all of Washington — from the United States Congress to the Chamber of Commerce — prepared to welcome him.

Below
Grahame-White lands his Farman biplane
on a street next to the White House

Right
Harriet Quimby, America's first licensed woman pilot
flew the English Channel in 1912

Finally a plane appeared in the sky and when it reached the city it circled and came down low along the broad streets. Instead of landing, however, it climbed back into the sky and disappeared. Reaction was puzzled and angry: what kind of a joke was this? The next morning newspapers had the answer. The plane was flown by a young Army lieutenant who thought he'd give the capital a show by flying down from the Signal Corps training field at College Park, Md. The jokester's name was Henry H. Arnold, later a five-star general in the Army Air Force. Atwood did appear a few days later, after unscheduled stops in Atlantic City and Baltimore, and received the personal congratulations of President Taft. The next month Harry Atwood flew for the money ($10,000 put up by Victor J. Evans, a Washington, D.C., patent attorney) and set a new long distance record of 1,155 miles from St. Louis to New York. The mark was wiped off the books four months later by Cal Rodgers' transcontinental flight.

Good money was to be had, too, in exhibitions that began to crop up all over the nation at country fairs, racetracks and cow pastures. This was barnstorming in its infancy, when the stunts and aerial maneuvers weren't so complicated as they later became, but when a pilot could produce gasps of wonder by merely getting his plane off the ground.

A sharp promoter could line up sizable crowds to see the flying fools risk their necks. The air above, though, was not the only hazard. The crowd on the ground sometimes got carried away with excitement and after a good show would happily tear off souvenir pieces of fabric from the airplanes. If the audience didn't like the show — or if they thought there wasn't going to be one held — they often weren't so happy. Ticket holders could work up an ugly mood if high winds or rain threatened to cancel. Even the early exhibition flyers had little stomach for foul weather flying.

Flyer Beckwith Havens was hauled out to his plane on a sheriff's buckboard after an angry crowd demanded he stop stalling for time. Havens feared stiff winds that day, but he flew anyway. Art Smith, the daring "Smashup Kid" of countless exhibitions, got out of a Texas town one rainy day in 1912 just in time to escape a furious crowd which thought it had been swindled. It seems the crate for Smith's airplane had *Honeybug* stenciled on it, the craft's name, and the citizenry had mistaken the word for "humbug." They thought it was the flyer's way of mocking them for a show he never intended to give.

The biggest names in exhibition aviation belonged to the traveling teams organized by Curtiss, the Wrights, and John Moisant. Curtiss' team boasted the great Beachey, Eugene Ely, Mars and Charles Willard. The Wrights' company starred Brookins, Arch Hoxsey, Coffyn and Ralph Johnstone. Moisant had an international team that included Roland Garros, the Frenchman who later became the first Allied "ace" of World War I.

Skilled though they were, aviators sometimes met their deaths flying fragile craft that were pushed beyond the limits of their capabilities. Ralph Johnstone had performed his famed "spiral glide" many times before

Left
Lincoln Beachey
at the controls of a Curtiss pusher

Opposite
Glenn L. Martin in his first airplane, a pusher
strongly modeled after Curtiss planes

thousands, but on Nov. 20, 1910, in Denver, Colo., the trick didn't work. His Wright biplane crumpled in its descent and crashed, killing Johnstone instantly. The Wrights lost another valued team member a month later when Arch Hoxsey, who once had taken ex-President Theodore Roosevelt up as a passenger, died in a crash at Dominguez Field, Los Angeles. The same day, Dec. 31, 1910, Moisant cracked up in New Orleans while landing in gusty winds. Moisant was well known for his pioneer Paris-to-London flight. His brother Alfred carried on the flying team but it was all over for the 35-year-old Chicagoan. He died on his way to the hospital.

Another shocker was the death of Harriet Quimby, a pretty, dark-haired magazine writer who became the "first woman to fly the English Channel" in April 1912. Back in America a few weeks later she met her death while flying in a meet at Boston.

Death did not come to the most colorful of them all, the "incomparable" Lincoln Beachey, until 1915, but into his comparatively few years of flying this short, stocky Californian with the jutting jaw packed a lifetime of fantastic feats. Beachey became a name in dirigible flying before he learned to fly airplanes. He had piloted Thomas Baldwin's airship at St. Louis in 1904 shortly after it made its first flight in Oakland, and he had established something of a record in 1906 by making the first airship flight around the Washington Monument. When he did get around to learning about airplanes in 1910 it looked for a while as if it would be a lost cause. Curtiss, at whose school he learned, had to turn away when Beachey left the ground. His early landings were best described as a series of controlled crashes. But he quickly learned, and soon became the star of the Curtiss exhibition team. Beachey flew through hangars, picked up handkerchiefs with his wing tips, and looped

the loop with his hands outstretched like a bird. In 1911 he flew under the Suspension Bridge at Niagara Falls and his races with racecar driver Barney Oldfield were the sensation of the day. "Linc" Beachey's most famous stunt was his "dive of death," in which he would make a vertical descent from 6,000 feet with his engine shut off, and land on a dime. Performing it, he learned how to conquer the dreaded tailspin by diving more steeply instead of trying to nose up.

Even though he had his share of mishaps Beachey seemed to lead a charmed life. He cracked up several times while racing Oldfield but walked away each time. Once while flying through a huge exhibition hall he hooked his wing tip on the exit door; the plane was a shambles but once more Beachey walked away. Another time, while buzzing a hangar his wing struck and killed a young woman standing on the roof.

On March 14, 1915, Beachey's luck ran out. For the San Francisco Exposition that year he had built a monoplane of his own design, powered by an 80-horsepower Gnome rotary engine and named the "Lincoln Beachey Special." The first time he took up the sleek little ship he thrilled the crowd with all the tricks he knew. The second time he went into his show stopper, the death dive. This time he didn't recover. Perhaps unused to the new plane's controls or its higher speed he plunged straight into San Francisco Bay. His body was found in 60 feet of water, trapped in the wreckage of the silver and yellow plane.

Commenting on the tragedy, Howard Huntington, an American Aero Club official, predicted that Beachey's death would put "an end to daredevil flying." He was only half right. It lapsed for a few years, but came back stronger than ever during the 1920s and '30s. Beachey's spectacular dive was an end, all right, but only of an era.

5
Growing Pains

What was an airplane for? Was it just an exhibition gimmick, a sportsman's pleasure? Or was it the vehicle of the future, opening a new path of navigation through the skies?

Those were questions many were asking as the first decade of flight wore on. In warfare a clear role for the airplane was foreseen by some in reconnaissance and observation; a few early prophets also saw its use as the deadly bomb and gun carrier it would later become. Several European nations, most notably France, were beginning to develop airplanes for military use before the outbreak of World War I. Yet top brass in the United States refused to follow suit; they scorned the airplane as a freak, or else feared it would upset their traditional warfare.

Ten years after Kitty Hawk even less progress was being made toward commercial aviation. Passenger-carrying stunts abounded,

such as the 1912 trip pilot Frank Coffyn made down New York Bay to put a tardy passenger aboard a transatlantic liner. But it was not until 1914 that the first scheduled airline was established anywhere in the world, and then the venture was short-lived. P.E. Fansler's airline used a Benoist flying boat to cover the 22-mile route between St. Petersburg and Tampa, Florida, with Tony Jannus as the pilot. A few others picked up the idea, but commercial aviation would have to wait until the 1920's to come to life.

Progress in air mail was almost as feeble. The first recorded delivery of mail by air in the United States was made in 1911 during an international aviation tournament in Garden City, Long Island, New York. Army Capt. Paul W. Beck, accompanied by the Postmaster General of the United States in a Curtiss biplane, and stunt flyer Earle R.

The 1912 Gallaudet *Bullet*
showed aerodynamic sophistication
and great speed

Ovington piloting a Queen monoplane (an American copy. of a Blériot), flew to Mineola some 10 miles away and dropped small mail pouches. But from that event until the establishment of regular airmail service in May 1918 the delivery of letters by air was largely in the hands of the exhibition flyers. Aviation meets often featured short airmail hops authorized by the Post Office Department, or staged mail-dropping contests for accuracy.

Octave Chanute, the engineer, glider builder and friend of the Wrights, had once predicted that airplanes would "make all parts of the globe accessible, bring men into closer relation with each other, advance civilization, and hasten the promised era in which there shall be nothing but peace and good will among all men." Chanute's words were far from being realized 10 years after practical flight had been achieved.

What was delaying progress? For one thing, there was the refusal of military seniors already mentioned to accept the airplane innovation. For another there was no organized effort in the United States — military or otherwise — to research and develop aircraft. France, Germany, Great Britain and Italy had aeronautical research operations as early as 1909, but the United States had nothing similar until 1913 when the Smithsonian Institution briefly reopened Samuel Langley's old laboratory. Courses in aerodynamics could be taken at two or three universities, but whatever continuing encouragement there was for aviation came from the private-member Aero Club of America, not from government sources.

Also hindering aviation advances was the bitter patent fight that broke out over the Wrights' claim that their wing-warping device was the basic control system and that other methods, specifically the aileron rig used by Curtiss, were merely extensions of their invention. The court battle stretched over

several years and lined up powerful financial interests on each side: J.P. Morgan, backing the Wrights and a combination of Bell, Henry Ford and the old Langley supporters at the Smithsonian behind Curtiss. The woolly legalisms at issue, plus the prospect of a fight with powerful financiers, discouraged some of the nation's most imaginative minds.

There were some bright spots, to be sure. Easily the most outstanding of the early American workers, other than the Wrights and Curtiss, was Glenn L. Martin. This ramrod straight, bespectacled dynamo of a man was talented as a flyer, engineer and businessman. Born in Iowa in 1886, he followed the classic route to aviation through work with bicycles and automobiles. He built his first airplane in 1908, a pusher biplane that looked and operated much like Curtiss' craft of the same period. But he soon forged his own path, gathering around him some of the best engineering talent in the country. In 1913 he built a "Model T" tractor-propeller biplane which in its modified version ("TT") became what has been called the Army's first really safe and satisfactory training plane. The TT had a 90-horsepower Curtiss OX-2 engine and interplane ailerons favored by Curtiss. A later type, the Model S, was powered by a 125-horsepower Hall-Scott engine, had upper wing ailerons, and was fitted with floats.

Martin made airplanes for private use, too, among them a rotary-engine biplane for Lincoln Beachey's use, and a four-passenger seaplane built for ferrying passengers in Oregon.

Prominent as a manufacturer of early military planes was the Burgess Company of Marblehead, Mass., which liked to use Wright or Curtiss features in its products. The company's model H, a biplane with wing-warping controls and a 70-horsepower Renault engine, was purchased by the Army in 1912 and became its first tractor design. A Burgess seaplane, the *Flying Fish*, sported twin floats

The Navy's first airplane,
a Curtiss "Triad," with Curtiss at the controls
and Navy Lt. Ellyson as a passenger

and a 30-horsepower engine spinning a pusher prop, and was used by the Army in 1915 in the Philippines. The Navy bought several Burgess-Dunne tailless biplanes in 1913. Radical in appearance, they were among the first "swept wing" airplanes and although without tail assembly, they achieved longitudinal stability by placement of elevators well aft of the center of gravity. They were driven by a 200-horsepower Canton-Unne water-cooled radial engine and pusher prop.

Other pre-war manufacturers included the Sturtevant Aeroplane Co. of Boston, which made trainers and observation biplanes; the Sloan Aircraft Co., Inc., later becoming the Standard Aero Corp., maker of reconnaissance biplanes; the L.W.F. Engineering Co., Inc., of College Point, Long Island, another observation-trainer manufacturer; Tom Benoist, whose company in St. Louis, Mo., turned out the world's first scheduled airliners; and Frank E. Boland, whose own flying boat took its builder to his death.

An adventurous design turned out by the Gallaudet Engineering Co. was the *Bullet,* a streamlined monoplane with engine enclosed in the nose and pusher propeller in the tail. It was supposedly tested at 100 miles an hour.

European aviation showed greater willingness to experiment during the pre-war period. The French distinguished themselves especially in the monoplane field with machines built by Blériot, Lavavasseur, Esnault-Pelterie, Nieuport, Morane, Hanriot, and Deperdussin. In 1912 the monocoque (single shell) fuselage was introduced in the Deperdussin monoplane, giving it a clean, modern appearance well ahead of any other design of the period. In this plane, powered by a 140-horsepower Gnome rotary, Jules Vedrines won the 1912 Gordon Bennett in Chicago with a new world's speed record.

But the promising development of monoplanes was interrupted at about this time

after two of them crashed, with the result that a temporary ban was placed on this type in France and England. Attention returned to the biplane which, with materials and knowledge then available, was the more reliable type.

The most glowing chapter in American aviation just prior to World War I concerns Glenn Curtiss' development of seaplanes. As we have seen, Curtiss had experimented on Keuka Lake with *Loon,* which was nothing more than a pontoon-carrying *June Bug.* By 1910 his mind turned toward two separate possibilities, each of which became the seed for two great branches of naval aviation. One led to the birth of aircraft carriers, the other to the development of flying boats and their smaller seaplane sisters.

The carrier concept was born when Navy Capt. Washington I. Chambers, the first Navy aviation chief, arranged for an 83-foot, forward-sloping flight deck to be built on the cruiser U.S.S. *Birmingham.* Curtiss supplied the plane as well as the civilian pilot, Eugene Ely, a graduate of the Curtiss flying school and one of the most famous of the aerial daredevils. Ely took off from the deck on Nov. 14, 1910, as the ship was anchored at the mouth of Chesapeake Bay. The biplane's wheels appeared to touch water briefly, but it recovered and went on to land near Norfolk, Virginia.

Curtiss pilot, Eugene Ely, lands his plane
on an improvised deck
aboard the U.S.S. *Pennsylvania*

Two months later Curtiss, Ely and the U.S. Navy went a step further. This time a 125-foot flight platform was installed on the stern of the U.S.S. *Pennsylvania*. As thousands of sailors cheered from a fleet of ships in San Francisco Bay, Ely soared in for another "first" — this time a landing. Fifty-seven minutes later he took off again and Navy flattops were born.

Working in another direction, Curtiss equipped one of his standard biplanes with pontoons and flew it from his flying school at North Island, San Diego, Calif., out to the anchored *Pennsylvania* where it was hauled aboard, then lowered again for a return flight to land. The brief operation satisfied the Secretary of the Navy's suggestion that a seaplane should be able to light on the water and be hoisted aboard a warship, but improvements would have to be made before Curtiss' "hydroaeroplane," as it was called, was a practical aircraft. A particularly knotty problem was the shape of the hull or pontoons. Curtiss' first flat bottomed designs clung maddeningly to the water before they became unstuck — if they lifted at all. After numerous experiments a step was built to break the water's suction and takeoffs became easier.

Meantime, the Navy was forming its own aerial unit. Three aviators were trained, Lt. Theodore G. Ellyson, who received the permanent designation of Naval Aviator No. 1; Lt. John Rodgers, and Lt. (jg) John H. Towers. On May 8, 1911, Capt. Chambers took steps to buy the Navy's first airplane, a Curtiss designated A-1 but popularly called the "Triad." Specifications were for a speed of 45 m.p.h., a 75-horsepower engine and two seats side by side with controls at both positions. Curtiss had tested a prototype in February but tested the Navy's plane himself in July, taking it up only 25 feet. He went a little higher with Ellyson as passenger, and

The *America,*
another Curtiss achievement, ushered
in a long era of graceful flying boats

then the Navy's first aviator flew solo. Navy aviation was in business.

The Triad handled clumsily but it sparked a number of experimental "firsts." Equipped with wheels as well as floats, it made aviation's first amphibious trip, with Curtiss taking off from land, lifting its wheels in flight and landing on water. It also was flown by Ellyson for the first night flight made by a naval aviator. And on Sept. 7 it got off a crude kind of catapult by sliding down a wire grooved along the hull bottom, wobbling into the air.

The next year saw more intensive work on the catapult idea. Ellyson got a dunking but was uninjured when he tried to catapult off a battleship in a Curtiss AH-3. Toward the end of 1912 a number of successful launchings had been made with a compressed air catapult devised by Capt. Chambers, Naval Constructor Holden C. Richardson and Lt. St. Clair Smith of the Naval Gun Factory.

Curtiss pushed his seaplane refinements further ahead during 1912 by building his first real flying boat. Cleanly designed for its day with a highly polished wooden veneer hull, the Curtiss boat was sold mainly to private sportsmen although the Army and Navy also made purchases. It had pilots seated side by side in a cockpit built in the hull — an innovation for Curtiss whose previous designs had their airmen taking the full blast of the wind. A Curtiss V-8 engine rated at about 80 horsepower spun the pusher prop, and interplane ailerons were employed.

Variations of the flying boat followed in 1913-14, one of them a monoplane, another a four-passenger model bearing such unheard of luxuries as a tachometer, air speed indicator, barometer and clock.

Curtiss' 1914 work centered on two projects, one an attempt to hit back at the Wrights' legal offensive by proving the old Langley *Aerodrome* could fly after all (thus

discrediting the brothers' claim they were first to fly), and the other, the flying boat *America* which was to make the first transatlantic flight. The revival of the old *Aerodrome* was a sorry episode in the Hammondsporter's life, for although it rose off Keuka Lake it was later found that many modifications had been made.

Curtiss' *America,* financed by the Philadelphian Rodman Wanamaker and to be piloted by the Englishman J.C. Porte, was an enclosed cabin biplane that mounted twin OX engines and wore the sturdy look of a trans-ocean winner. But the fuel needed for the long trip weighed more than the craft could manage. Before a solution could be found World War I broke out, precluding an Atlantic attempt until another Curtiss boat spanned the ocean five years later.

In spite of the contributions of Curtiss and a handful of brilliant engineers and dedicated manufacturers, Army and Navy aerial progress was moving at a snail's pace. When Germany marched against France in August 1914 the United States had on hand a total of 23 airplanes for naval or military use. France had 1,400, Germany 1,000, Russia 800 and Great Britain 400.

Ironically, it was the nation weakest in aircraft — the United States — which was the first to experiment with the airplane as a practical military instrument.

6
Taste of Battle

On March 3, 1911, a Wright B biplane took off from a bumpy dirt field in Laredo, Texas, with two men aboard. At the controls was Philip O. Parmalee, a civilian pilot trained by the Wright brothers, and serving as observer was Lt. Benjamin D. Foulois, one of the United States Army's first airplane pilots. Parmalee and Foulois climbed to about 1,200 feet and headed northwest toward Eagle Pass, 106 miles away. They were making the first military reconnaissance by airplane in history — a fact that probably concerned them less than the hazards at hand. As they peered below looking for "enemy" troops in the Army maneuvers being staged along the border of Mexico, they shuddered at the rugged, rocky terrain along the Rio Grande River passing beneath them. Each time their chugging engine backfired they wondered what landing on that treacherous surface would be like.

Once on the ground at Eagle Pass they took stock. They had completed one leg of their mission, an accomplishment in itself considering their machine and the conditions in which they were operating. They had failed to spot the "enemy," but on the other hand this knowledge alone was of strategic value to their side in the war "games" they were playing. They also had chalked up another "first" on the trip by making military use of an airborne radio. Foulois had had a small radio installed in the plane by which he communicated his findings to Signal Corps stations along the border.

On their return trip to Fort McIntosh in Laredo, the two flyers weren't so fortunate. About 25 miles out of Eagle Pass, Parmalee, acting this time as observer, saw some ducks and in a frolicsome mood pretended to take a shotgun bead on them. In lifting his arms he accidentally tripped the engine cutout; the Wright biplane abruptly nosed down and crashed into the Rio Grande, temporarily

pinning its human cargo under it. Faced for a few moments with the prospect of drowning, Foulois and Parmalee managed to wriggle out — wet, angry and reasonably unharmed. Just as they were preparing for a long, hot walk back to Eagle Pass a Texas cowboy hailed them. He was dispatched back to camp where he notified the commander of the flyers' predicament. Men and machine were hauled ingloriously back in a horse and wagon.

Army aviation was still an infant less than two years old when Foulois and Parmalee made that Texas flight. The Army had purchased its first airplane on Aug. 3, 1909, after a series of tests at Fort Myer, Va. As part of the same purchase contract, the Wrights trained two men as the first Army pilots, Lt. Frederic E. Humphreys and Lt. Frank P. Lahm. But within a few months each was ordered back to previous duties; Humphreys with the Corps of Engineers and Lahm with the Cavalry. Benny Foulois became the lone "pilot" in the Army's aviation arm (then under the Signal Corps). Benny had flown with the Wrights as a passenger but had never actually taken over the controls. Foulois almost immediately was ordered to move Aeroplane No. 1 and nine mechanics from College Park, Md., where they had

Reconnaissance flight over the Rio Grande. Observer on that flight was Lt. Benjamin Foulois (photo opposite), who became chief of the Air Corps in the 1930's

established themselves, to the warmer climate of Fort Sam Houston, Texas. Brig. Gen. James Allen, the Chief Signal Officer, ordered Foulois to "take plenty of spare parts, and teach yourself to fly."

Foulois, with a determination that was to land him the job of Air Corps Chief during the 1930's, did teach himself to fly—although strictly along trial and error lines. All in one day he made his first solo, takeoff, landing and crash, luckily without injury. On another occasion a Texas wind gust slapped his Wright biplane to the ground, inflicting on the little pilot a severe cut of the left leg. It left the only visible scar Foulois carried in his long and active aviation career.

Foulois had other concerns besides his own education as a flyer. He soon found himself contributing his own money to maintain the much-damaged Aeroplane No. 1, as he had

been allotted only $150 for such purposes. He also was given added duties of setting up a complicated electrical buzzer system on a firing range 25 miles away, but managed, nevertheless, to rig a tricycle landing gear and make other improvements on the Army's only airplane despite the extra work. Foulois had encountered severe bucking in the Wright Model A, and had to devise a seat belt to hold himself down. He wrote the Wrights about the plane's instability problems, with the result that the brothers eliminated their forward elevator system in their next model.

It was in this modified Wright B, loaned to the Army by the wealthy magazine publisher Robert F. Collier, that Foulois and Parmalee made their reconnaissance flight from Laredo to Eagle Pass. It was a red-letter day for Army aviation, for on the same date Congress appropriated $125,000

for aeronautics — the first such appropriation ever — and Gen. Allen promptly ordered five new airplanes, three of them Wrights and Two Curtiss biplane pushers.

The arrival of the first Curtiss, designated Aeroplane No. 2, did not exactly herald a new era for Army aviation. It created an unforeseen problem in that it had a different control system from the Wright, and accommodation for only one pilot at the controls (the Wrights sat its flyers side by side at dual controls). This meant that pilots trained on the Wright could not easily switch to the Curtiss and so there developed a rivalry between the Wright pilots — Foulois and, by now, civilian Frank Coffyn — and the Curtiss flyers, Lt. Paul W. Beck, Lt. G.E.M. Kelly and Lt. John C. Walker. Kelly was later killed in No. 2 and Walker quit flying after nearly crashing.

Nevertheless Army aviation moved ahead, albeit slowly. In September 1911 Army Lt. Thomas Milling won distinction at a Boston air meet by flying at night. A year and a half later he set a new American two-man duration and distance record with Lt. William C. Sherman by flying 200 miles over Texas in four hours and 22 minutes. Paul Beck had invented a crude bombsight which was demonstrated at the Los Angeles air meet in 1910, and the following year Riley E. Scott, a former Coast Artillery officer, showed Army brass at College Park, Md., an improved bombsight which zeroed in 18-pound bombs within 10 feet of a target. Other firsts included the establishment by the Army of the first overseas air base in the spring of 1912, in the Philippines, and the testing of the newly invented Lewis machine gun on a Wright biplane at College Park. The first Army tractor-prop plane (a Burgess) also was acquired in 1912.

Army aviation carried out the first military mission with its Foulois-Parmalee reconnais-sance flight of 1911, but it was the Navy whose aviators were to experience the first enemy gunfire (though not in history; Italian airplane pilots had heard the whine of bullets late in 1911 and early the next year in the Italo-Turkish War). In the spring of 1914 a new government in Mexico arrested U.S. sailors in Vera Cruz, and U.S. Naval and Marine forces prepared to move into the city in retaliation. Sailing with the assault force on the cruiser *Mississippi* were a Curtiss hydroaeroplane and a Curtiss flying boat to be manned for observation purposes by Lt. (jg) Patrick N.L. Bellinger and three student pilots. Another cruiser, the *Birmingham,* had three aircraft aboard commanded by Lt. John H. Towers, but it was Bellinger and his observer, Lt. (jg) Dick Saufley, who got a taste of battle. Flying over the outskirts of the city on May 6 in search of enemy gun emplacements, the Navy flyers were startled to see rifle slugs ripping through the plane's fabric. They were unhurt and the plane was easily patched after it had been thoroughly examined by curious sailors.

Army airmen, itching to get into action during the Vera Cruz incident, had to wait until 1916 to get their baptism of fire. Again Mexico was involved, except that this time tension between the two nations was touched off by the bandit activities of the revolutionary Francisco "Pancho" Villa along the border. When Villa and his band of revolutionaries struck the town of Columbus, New Mexico, on March 9, 1916, killing 17 Americans, President Woodrow Wilson ordered American troops under Brig. Gen. John J. Pershing in hot pursuit of the bandit.

Even before Villa's raid into American territory, Army airmen had come close to being called on for reconnaissance chores as the Mexican's operations along the border were getting too close for comfort. But the aviators were stymied by the diplomatic limits

Curtiss "Jennies," with engines covered against sandstorms at Ojo Federico, Mexico

imposed on them, and found that the grueling weather conditions along the border made getting planes aloft difficult.

Eight Curtiss JN-2's (early "Jenny" types) received by the First Aero Squadron in 1915 were an improvement over the Burgesses, Wrights and open-frame Curtiss biplanes operating until then, but in spite of high hopes held for their performance, they proved unequal to the task of flying regularly in the hot, dry Southwest. Modifications were made to replace rudder controls (ailerons were operated with a shoulder-yoke) and various faulty parts. Six of the modified types (now designated JN-3) winged their way from Fort Sill, Okla., to a new base at Fort Sam Houston, Texas, a distance of 439 miles. The laboriously made journey pointed up the deficiencies of the "Jennies", but they were the best the Army had. A few months later Villa struck Columbus and the First Aero Squadron was ordered to entrain for New Mexico to join Pershing's Punitive Expedition.

The Army's tiny aerial force — it consisted at the outset of the expedition of eight "Jennies" and 10 pilots under the command of Foulois — operated under severe hardship during the Mexican expedition and scored few real accomplishments. The actual period of practical operations lasted no more than six weeks. Yet the force won admiration for its determination and bravery, and the difficulty it encountered alerted Army top brass to the neglect aviation had endured.

The Squadron made at least one effective reconnaissance mission from its first base at Columbus, but a few days after it was established there the group was ordered to Casas Grandes south of the border to be closer to Pershing's fast-moving cavalry columns. The flight from Columbus to the new camp almost turned into disaster when planes strayed off course, turned back or crashed. When they finally regrouped they managed to make

a number of reconnaissance and message- or mail-carrying flights but all against the greatest of odds. The "Jennies" weren't designed for flights much beyond 50 miles from base; wind and sandstorms were a constant impediment to engines and controls; the planes often couldn't rise above high hills; propellers warped and cracked in the arid climate; hostile villagers turned flights for supplies into life-risking ventures.

Foulois and Lt. Herb A. Dargue had a narrow escape on one supply-seeking trip to Chihuahua when crowds surrounded their plane on landing, took Foulois hostage and threw him in jail. Dargue took off again and escaped, only to see his plane slashed with knives by angry citizens when he landed again a few miles away. The American consul came to the hapless flyers' rescue, and after they had spent a night at the consulate building, they left the next morning in their hastily patched airplane. Another harrowing tale to come out of the Punitive Expedition involved the crash of two pilots while on a reconnaissance mission, and their forced hike back to San Antonio, Mexico, a span of 65 miles. When they reached the base, one of the airmen, Lt. R. H. Willis, was told by doctors he had hobbled all the way on a broken ankle. He replied that must have been why he felt so much better sitting than standing on his feet.

At Foulois' insistence, the Army sent four new Curtiss N-8's to the First Squadron. Duplicates of the JN-4's which were then being delivered as trainers to Allied forces overseas, the 8's had 90-horsepower engines — slightly more powerful than the Squadron's tired JN-3's. However, Foulois found them as inadequate as the 3's and told Gen. Pershing so. More powerful Curtiss R-2's, fitted with the Curtiss VX 150-horsepower engine, were shipped next, but they too failed to meet rigorous tests under prevailing conditions.

41

The Curtiss JN-4, popularly called "Jenny,"
was used to train pilots in World War I.
The "Jenny" had an extended career lasting
until the 1930's

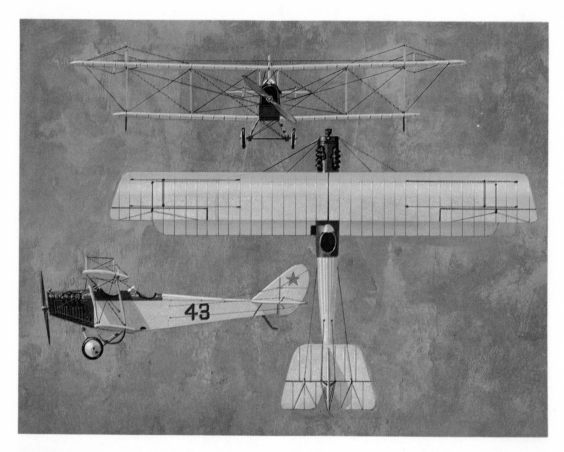

Mechanical bugs constantly cropped up and propellers remained a problem in their failure to endure the extremes of heat and aridity. An improved version, the R-4 equipped with a 200-horsepower Curtiss V-2 engine, was then sent, and one twin-engine Curtiss, tentatively designated the JN-5, was employed for a time by the Squadron. But by summer operations began to peter out as Pershing's forces failed to locate the elusive Villa. The Punitive Expedition ended 11 months after it started without catching the bandit.

Although aviation played a minor role in the Punitive Expedition, its supporters could point to several genuine contributions. In several instances, it had made observations across territory where no one else — not infantry or cavalry — could operate. It ran messages and it carried mail. It logged 346 hours of flying time on 540 missions and covered more than 19,533 miles doing so. Its performance emphasized certain glaring weaknesses which obviously needed correction. And it spurred some new thinking in the isolation-minded United States about aviation's role in warfare: By December 1916 seven Army air squadrons were active or in the process of being organized, with six additional reserve squadrons under recommendation for coastal defense. Congress that same year made its first important appropriation for military aviation — $13,281,666.

The awakening was slowly coming if indeed it was not already too late.

7
Lafayette Escadrille

Every war has its heroes, those figures of bravery and courage who give the bloody business of killing some redeeming quality. World War I had its own large collection of heroes, for not only was it a long war, lasting more than four years, but it was an especially brutal one. For the first time in history peoples from every part of the globe were involved, and new, mechanized weapons changed the whole character of warfare. When hostilities started in 1914, horse cavalry galloped to meet the foe; French soldiers trooped to the front dressed in proud red and blue uniforms, and officers brandished swords in the face of the enemy. At war's end in November 1918 such dashing vestiges of the past had given way to the grim realities of modern warfare. The cavalry had been replaced by tanks, uniforms were a dreary brown or gray, and soldiers huddled in deep trenches amidst the terrifying sounds of bombs, shells and machine guns.

High above the battle another new weapon made its debut. It was the airplane, a mere ten years old, but soon to make an indelible impression on the conduct of warfare. At first it was limited to observation use, and neither side interfered much with the other as it went about its business. This rapidly changed. Pistols, rifles, pieces of metal dangled on strings into the propellers of the enemy below — all were used in the first stages of the war to thwart an opponent's mission. By 1915 the game was turning deadly. Machine guns were mounted in observers' cockpits by the Germans, and the French aerial daredevil Roland Garros, now flying for his nation's *Aviation Militaire,* had a propeller of his plane fitted with steel deflection plates so that he could fire his machine gun through the whirling blades. The Germans did him one better by employing the Dutch aerial engineer Anthony Fokker to design an interrupter gear which synchronized machine gun-fire with the propeller so that bullets would avoid the blades. By this time airplanes had already proven their value as flying observation posts. Now they became deadly gun platforms as well. A new method of warfare, with its own tactics and weapons, had been born.

Equally as impressive to all those who read and heard about the air war were the men fighting it. Pilots were dubbed with such fanciful titles as the "Knights of the Blue"; the names of individual aces were known to every romantic young man who read about them. They gave a dash of glamour to an otherwise strange and ugly war. On the ground men were mere parts in the huge war machine that rolled back and forth across the trenches of northern France. Up in the skies, men fought as men — with a touch of skill and chivalry that reminded the world of the clashes between the armored knights of old.

America hastened to proclaim its neutrality at the outbreak of the war in 1914 but its melting pot population, with strong ties to Europe, could not very well stay indifferent to the struggle overseas. Although sentiment in some areas favored the Central Powers, an influential majority of the American people supported the Allies' cause. Even as the war broke out, volunteers rushed to enlist in Allied units like the Foreign Legion which did not require them to give up U.S. citizenship. A few young men, entranced with the stories they had heard about flying, signed up with Britain's Royal Flying Corps or, when openings occurred, the French Army's air service. From these French aerial units would come the first all-American fighting outfit in the war — the Lafayette Escadrille.

From the moment the Lafayette Escadrille went into action it was a living legend. As a pursuit or "chasse" squadron it turned in a creditable record of 39 victories, but it was not the number of enemy kills that made it so fascinating to the folks at home. What

stirred interest was a natural desire to see
the first American outfit acquit itself well.
The off-duty escapades of this hard-drinking,
hard-playing band of adventurers who kept a
couple of lion cubs as mascots also thrilled
newspaper readers at home. It is questionable
if the Lafayette Escadrille influenced the
United States to enter the war, as the French
hoped it would, but there is no doubt that it
inspired large numbers of individual young
Americans to enlist in air service. And equally
as important, the Lafayette Escadrille and its
sister organization which included all the
American flyers in other French squadrons,
the Lafayette Flying Corps, became the nu-
cleus of experienced leadership for the fledgling American Air Service when it was
girding for action late in the war.

For a while after the outbreak of the war
it seemed to those interested in forming an
American flying squadron that such a group
would never get off the ground. A number of
Yank flyers were sprinkled through French
escadrilles, but the French showed no enthusiasm for placing them in a single unit,
chiefly because there were more volunteers
for the air service than it needed. Two developments helped change the French authorities' minds, however. One was the determination of a few American flying enthusiasts
to see the creation of their own squadron.
The other was a massive German offensive
against Verdun. The French, battling for
survival, were persuaded that an American
aerial unit could help bring the United States
to the aid of the Allies.

The Lafayette Escadrille was inspired by
a wealthy Harvard law graduate, Norman
Prince, who had lived in France with his
family and knew some influential French
officials. Prince gained help from a few of
his well-to-do friends as well as from Dr.
Edmund Gros, a Paris-based American phy-
sician who was one of the leaders of the

American Ambulance Service. It turned out
that Gros also had dreamed of forming an
American squadron, and together Gros and
Prince worked to convince French authorities
of the value of their idea. The French con-
sented but let months go by without taking
action. Then in February 1916 the Germans
launched their attack on Verdun. On March
21, 1916, the *Escadrille Americaine* — as it
was initially called — came into being. One
month later, on April 20, the squadron went
into combat.

Seven pilots made up the charter group.
Prince was joined by Elliott Cowdin and
Victor Chapman, two other Harvardians,
and by William Thaw II, the son of a wealthy
Pittsburgh family who three years earlier had
quit his studies at Yale to concentrate on
flying. Kiffen Rockwell had fought with the
Foreign Legion before becoming a pilot, and
so had W. Bert Hall. James McConnell had
traded driving ambulances for piloting a war-
bird. The same mixture of backgrounds, with
a strong dash of wealthy ex-collegians, prevailed as new members were added. All had
a love of adventure, all had the desire to
fight the hated "Hun" from the cockpit of an
airplane.

The vanguard group was soon joined by
others whose names are prominent in Lafayette Escadrille history: Raoul Lufbery, Clyde
Balsley, Dudley Hill, Edmond Genet and
Courtney Campbell. Still later the Lafayette
roster added Edwin "Ted" Parsons, Kenneth
Marr, Harold Willis and James Norman Hall
(no relation to Bert Hall) to mention a few
of the 43 men who flew with the squadron.

A French officer, Capt. Georges Thenault, had the unenviable task of commanding
the Escadrille. The Americans had little interest in rules and regulations right from the
start. They were given the same training
French aviators received, breaking in on
clipped-wing Blériots (dubbed "Penguins")

Nieuport 17's, shown here on the flight line, were popular with American pilots

and advancing to aging Caudron G-3's. But the Yank flyers had their own way of doing things once they had their own squadron. The Americans received special treatment through a French policy which made them exempt from the normal disciplinary rules of the French air service. So Lafayette pilots could, and sometimes did, ignore Thenault's carefully worked out plans and fly off on their own with guns blazing, confident that they would not receive punishment for it.

The Lafayette flyers enjoyed favored treatment in a number of other ways. Uniforms were given only passing attention, and pocket money was never scarce because an American committee backed by multi-millionaire William K. Vanderbilt Sr. and his wife saw to it that each pilot received a hundred francs a month plus a reward of 500 francs for each aerial victory. At one point the Escadrille employed a cook from a fancy New York hotel to prepare meals which made the squadron's mess the most popular on the Western Front with visiting brass and pilots from other squadrons. The Lafayette's first base was in Luxeuil-les-Bains, a plush resort 40 miles from the front, where they lived in a villa and ate sumptuous meals at a nearby hotel. Kiffen Rockwell wrote his mother soon after that the men "live like princes."

The lives of the Lafayette airmen weren't always as glamourous as they seemed, however. American reporters, eager to infuse their dispatches home with excitement and adventure, often exaggerated the Lafayette's exploits. The Escadrille never again enjoyed the luxury of their first base at Luxeuil. Soon after going into combat the squadron was thrown into heavy fighting over Verdun. And when it was not involved in bitter plane-to-plane combat with German *Jagdstaffeln*, the Lafayette spent much of its duty time just like other squadrons in the French air service making dreary routine patrols, strafing trenches, escorting bombers and observation flights, and flying balloon-busting or low-level bombing missions.

The encounters of Lafayette pilots with the enemy provide some of the best air stories to come out of World War I. One of them stems from the squadron's participation in a big bombing raid in October 1916 on the Mauser rifle works in Germany and involves Didier Masson, a crackerjack pilot, who had been flying seven years when he joined the squadron. Masson was one of four Lafayette members escorting the mission together with a swarm of British Sopwith "1½ Strutter" two-seaters. The Lafayette's little Nieuports, more limited in range than the other planes, went to a point inside Germany and then swung back to refuel. The Americans rejoined the flight on its return from Germany, and for a while the trip home looked as if it would be uneventful. Suddenly a swarm of Fokker monoplanes swooped in, pouring bullets at the lumbering bombers. The Allied fighters paired off with the German attackers and soon the sky was filled with fierce dogfights. By this time, however, the Nieuports' fuel supplies were again running low. Masson was on the tail of a Fokker when his engine sputtered and quit. The dismayed airman put the plane into a long glide toward French lines and sat tight, praying. Now it was the Fokker's turn as it ripped machine-gun slugs through the American's windshield and instrument panel. Miraculously, Masson was unscathed. Then, unexpectedly, it was his own turn to attack as the German overshot the Nieuport and came within range of its guns. Masson squeezed off 20 rounds and the German plunged to earth. The American came down in French territory, jumped out and raced for a trench where wide-eyed poilus rewarded him with a drink.

One of the most hair-raising escapes in Lafayette annals involved James Norman

45

Hall, who later gained literary fame as co-author of *Mutiny on the Bounty*. Hall was a newcomer to the squadron when he climbed into his Spad to join a showcase patrol for visiting brass. As the rest of the flight taxied into position, Hall worked frantically to start his Spad, a hand-me-down machine of the variety usually assigned to fledglings. Patrol-leader Bill Thaw had anticipated engine trouble in Hall's plane, and had ordered him to hang back and cruise in the sky if he couldn't catch his comrades. But Hall had other ideas. After finally starting his reluctant machine, he winged off toward German lines looking for a fight. Spotting some specks in the distance, he rushed to join what he believed to be his own patrol. Once he slid into the formation he looked around — he was in the middle of a flight of enemy Albatros fighters! He went into frantic acrobatics but they proved of no use. The Germans poured streams of bullets at the hapless American. One slug grazed his head, another his groin and a third slammed into his left shoulder. The Spad spun down from 12,000 feet, its dazed pilot only dimly aware of what was happening. Then, near the ground, Hall's mind cleared and he hauled back on the stick. The riddled Spad, strained to the limits of its endurance, leveled off and glided gently into a first-line trench. In a streak of good fortune, the plane's wings caught the ridges of the trench, breaking its impact. Hall was dragged from his cockpit and rushed to a French hospital. Back at the Lafayette airdrome, his comrades heard of the accident and raced to the hospital where they expected to see Hall dead or dying. Instead they found the jaunty airman propped up in bed, reading a book of poetry.

Fatalities began cutting into the Lafayette two months after it entered combat. Victor Chapman was first to go, shot down as he flew a gift to a hospitalized friend. Kiffen Rockwell was next, the victim of a German Aviatik's rear-seat gunner. Then Norman Prince died in an emergency landing on an unfamiliar field. McConnell followed him to the grave after a vicious duel with enemy two-seaters. And Edmond Genet, who swore he would avenge McConnell's death, crashed from a shrapnel hit or sheer exhaustion — the cause was never officially determined. Soon after young Ronald Hoskier was gunned down while flying an ancient Morane parasol monoplane, a squadron favorite which the air service had ordered to be retired. Hoskier had insisted on taking it up one more time.

Lafayette pilots relaxing with mascot

Fortunately for Lafayette pilots, their standard flying mounts were more up-to-date than the obsolete Morane. They went into combat equipped with Nieuport 11's, tiny maneuverable biplanes that helped end the Fokker E-III monoplane "scourge" of 1915-16. By the fall of 1916 the squadron was flying Nieuport 17's, a larger, more powerful version of the 11 which could be fitted with a Vickers machine gun synchronized to fire through the prop (the earlier Nieuports had only a machine gun mounted above the top wing). In 1917 the Lafayette was given the Spad 7, the first version of the famed pursuit plane used by American Army squadrons toward the end of the war. The early Spad had a Hispano-Suiza engine developing up to 200 h.p. and was immediately liked by pilots for its speed and sturdiness. All the Lafayette airplanes had one characteristic in common, the "Whooping Indian" insignia retained by the squadron even after it transferred to the American Air Service.

The greatest individual star in the Escadrille was Raoul Lufbery, whose 17 official victories made him by far the squadron's highest scorer. (The two next highest, credited with three kills each, were Norman Prince and Lt. Alfred de Meux de Laage, assistant to squadron commander Thenault.) Short, muscular and quiet in manner, Lufbery epitomized the kind of tough, adventurous airmen who so captivated youngsters reading about them at home. A vagabond before the war who claimed Wallingford, Conn., as his home, Lufbery had soldiered with the Americans in the Philippines and had been a mechanic for an exhibition pilot named Marc Pourpe in the Orient. As a pilot himself, Lufbery had been slow to learn, but his zeal for flying and the care he took with his airplane soon made him one of the most respected aviators on the Western Front. On the ground "Luf" babied his planes and armament, inspecting every round of ammunition to insure against his guns jamming in action. In the air he often played a "loner" role and had a favorite trick of hiding in clouds and pouncing on stray enemy planes. But Lufbery was a good team pilot who saved his comrades from death on more than one occasion.

Courageous though he was, Lufbery had a strong fear of fire in an airplane. German pilots could bail out with parachutes; Allied airmen other than balloon observers were not so equipped. A burning airplane meant one of two hideous alternatives for its pilot — jump, or stick with the plane in hopes of avoiding the flames long enough to bring the

fire under control. Like other airmen, Lufbery had often discussed the possibilities of fire, weighing one choice against the other. On May 19, 1918, his plane flamed during a battle with a German two-seater and he had to make the decision.

Lufbery was a major in the 94th Squadron of the U.S. Air Service at this time, the Lafayette Escadrille having ceased operations under the French flag. He had been serving as a tutor to inexperienced American flyers when a German photographic plane appeared over his field that spring day. Lufbery reacted instinctively. His own plane was temporarily out of commission so he climbed into a combat-ready Nieuport 28 and roared off. Soon he overtook the German and opened fire, but his guns jammed on the first pass and he came around again, his guns now apparently cleared. Both planes traded gunfire, but this time the German rear-seat gunner found his mark and the whole front end of the Nieuport burst into flames. Although there were conflicting reports about what happened next, most witnesses believe that Lufbery climbed out of his cockpit toward the tail of the falling plane in an effort to dodge the fire. Then, they say, he jumped from a height of over 5,000 feet. His body landed in the backyard of a shoemaker's house in Maron, not far from the Moselle.

The end of the Lafayette Escadrille as a French unit became inevitable after America entered the war. On February 18, 1918, it became the 103rd Pursuit Squadron in the U.S. Air Service. Technically the transition was smooth, but many of the squadron's members didn't find the change easy. The commissions some expected became snarled in red tape, and the stiff regulations of American units didn't sit well with pilots accustomed to the more casual ways of the French.

American flyers who had served in other French squadrons, those who composed the Lafayette Flying Corps, experienced similar problems. Together with Lafayette Escadrille members, few qualified under the rigid physical requirements of the U.S.A.S. Lufbery at 32 was technically too old and Bill Thaw had impaired vision in one eye, plus bad hearing and a knee injury. Others had flat feet, chronic tonsilitis or various ailments that normally would disqualify them. Waivers finally had to be obtained from the man at the top, Gen. John J. Pershing.

Many of the Lafayette flyers, both from the Escadrille and the Flying Corps, went on to serve with distinction in new roles. Several became leaders of American squadrons, while others like Thaw and Dudley Hill of the Escadrille and Charles Biddle of the Flying Corps were made commanders of larger American pursuit groups. Frank Baylies and David Putnam, both former Flying Corps flyers, chalked up 12 victories each in American uniform before dying in combat. Combined, the Lafayette veterans made up a valuable pool of experienced airmen who helped guide newly arrived American pilots into the final phase of the war.

8
America Joins the Fight

America entered World War I on April 6, 1917, but one year passed before the Army's first air squadrons went into action. The Aviation Section of the Signal Corps, the Army's air arm, had only a handful of officers and men when the United States entered the war. Time was consumed training thousands of flyers, building training fields and organizing out of the old Signal Corps setup a United States Air Service which could cope with combat conditions in France. Delays also resulted from a bitter rivalry among top brass, and equipment was slow in coming to squadrons.

In spite of frustrations, the U.S. Air Service fought on the Western Front for seven months and became a first-class combat outfit by the time the Armistice was signed on November 11, 1918. The Air Service represented about 10 percent of Allied air strength at war's end and fielded 45 squadrons at the front in which there were 767 pilots, 481 observers and 23 aerial gunners. In addition, nearly 100 Americans flew Caproni bombers on the Italian front. Official records show that Americans claimed a three-to-one ratio of victories over their German opponents, accounting for 781 enemy aircraft and 73 balloons. On the debit side 289 American planes and 48 balloons were reported downed.

The Air Service officially went into action on April 14, 1918, the honor falling to the 94th Pursuit Squadron. The flyers assigned to that inaugural flight were perhaps a little more nervous than they might otherwise have been when the day dawned miserably cold and dangerously foggy. Visibility on the ground was limited to a few feet and was probably even worse upstairs. But the orders had been issued: a patrol would start at 6 a.m., climb to 16,000 feet and intercept any enemy aircraft that ventured across the front lines.

Three pilots were assigned — Capt. David Peterson and Lieutenants Reed Chambers and Edward Rickenbacker. They were among the best airmen in the 94th but they were up against the worst flying weather. Shortly after they took off Peterson turned back because of the thick fog, but Chambers and Rickenbacker continued on, believing Peterson had run into engine trouble. They soon became hopelessly lost and found their way back to the airdrome only with great difficulty. Soon after their return, an alarm was given that two enemy planes were approaching the squadron's base, and two officers assigned to backstop roles that morning, Lieutenants Douglas Campbell and Alan Winslow, took off in their Nieuport 28's. Within minutes both had nailed the German planes— a double victory on the Air Service's first day in combat! Winslow was credited with the first victory and Campbell the second.

If American airmen thought the enemy would be a pushover, they were quickly disillusioned by the tough fighting that followed. By the spring of 1918 the war had reached a critical turning point. Both sides were weary to the point of exhaustion after three and a half years of stalemate. The Allies had attempted to break the German grip on northern France in 1917 with massive attacks. In 1918 it became the turn of the Germans to make a big push in the knowledge that America's entry into the war would make victory impossible in another year. In March they drove deep into the British Army positions along the Somme, and in April they penetrated the British lines again at Ypres, their advance being stopped both times with great human sacrifice. Worried Allied leaders hurriedly met to choose a single commander to coordinate their beleaguered forces, naming Marshal Ferdinand Foch Commander-in-Chief of Allied Forces in France. In May the Germans concentrated new attacks on the French Armies in the southern sector of the

front. Driving south between Soissons and Rheims, the Germans penetrated to the Marne and turned toward Paris. At this crucial hour the American ground troops were thrown into the breech, helping stem the German advance at Château-Thierry.

American aero squadrons assigned to the relatively quiet Toul sector of the front found their breaking-in period suddenly curtailed. Taking to the air over heavy ground-fighting, they were pitted against some of the best squadrons the Germans had, including the famous *Jagdstaffel* 1, the red-nosed pursuit group formerly commanded by Baron von Richthofen. It was midsummer before American strength began to build up sufficiently to become a match for the veteran Boche squadrons. The 94th was joined in April by the 95th Pursuit Squadron and together the two comprised a hard-hitting First Pursuit Group. The old First Aero Squadron of Mexican border fame, now commanded by Major Ralph Royce, also went into action in April. In May three more pursuit squadrons, two observation and one bombing squadron began operations. In June five more squadrons entered combat.

By midsummer, too, American pursuit squadrons were beginning to receive the Spad 13, the fast, chunky, Hispano-Suiza powered biplane that could do 130 m.p.h. American pursuit units were originally equipped with the Nieuport 28, a graceful, quick-climbing plane which had one unfortunate characteristic: it tended to shed its wing fabric if dived too fast. The new Spads were not as maneuverable but they were preferred by most Yank aviators for their speed.

The inexperience of the Americans when they entered the fray is illustrated by an incident involving Eddie Rickenbacker, the U.S. "ace of aces" at the end of the war. Flying an unarmed practice flight over German lines in March, "Rick" experienced the gamut of beginner's emotions. He was appalled by the devastation below; anti-aircraft bursts frightened him; he thought he was going to be sick. But by the time his patrol headed for home he was confident that combat flying wouldn't be so difficult after all. It took Major Raoul Lufbery, the veteran Lafayette Escadrille pilot who had led the patrol, to set Rick straight. On landing, Lufbery asked Rickenbacker and the third member of the patrol, Captain Doug Campbell, if they had observed any other planes during the flight.

"No," said the rookies as nonchalantly as possible, "not a one."

"Listen," said Lufbery, shaking his head. "One formation of five Spads crossed under us before we passed the lines. Another flight of five Spads went by about 15 minutes later, five hundred yards away. Damn good thing they weren't Boches. And there were four German Albatroses ahead of us when we turned back and another enemy two-seater closer to us than that. You must learn to look around."

Rickenbacker would have better days ahead than that one. A well-known auto-racing driver before the war, he began his Army service as a chauffeur to top brass. What Rick really wanted, though, was aviation. Wangling entry into the flying center at Tours, he emerged after 25 hours of flight time with his wings and a first lieutenancy. Superiors were more impressed with his mechanical ability, however, and sent him to the American air base and replacement depot at Issoudun as an engineering officer. Rickenbacker managed to get into active flying in the 94th by faking an illness to show he wasn't indispensible at Issoudun.

Rickenbacker was a methodical flyer who took few chances and more than two weeks passed before he downed his first German. Flying with James Norman Hall, like Luf-

Frank Luke, one of the hottest American pilots, downed four planes and fourteen balloons in seventeen days

bery a veteran of the Lafayette Escadrille, Rickenbacker met a German Pfalz fighter. The Americans zeroed in with Rick making the first pass, and then Hall. While the enemy tried to dodge his teammate, Rickenbacker caught the Pfalz with a burst of bullets. Before the Armistice Rickenbacker added 25 more victories to his score to register the top American tally. What made "Captain Eddie's" record particularly remarkable was the fact that he made it in only about two months of actual flying time at the front. Through much of the summer he was hospitalized with an ear infection and couldn't get back into action until September. By the time the war ended, though, he was the commander of the 94th and a hero to Americans back home. He was eventually awarded a Congressional Medal of Honor for his bravery, although it took Congress twelve years to do so.

American participation in the air war produced a number of heroes besides Rickenbacker. The most flamboyant of them was Frank Luke, the "balloon buster" from Arizona who died a storybook death holding off surrounding Germans with his pistol. Luke's record was as fully remarkable in its way as Rickenbacker's was in his, but where Rickenbacker was disciplined and patient, Luke was an aerial wild man who took tremendous risks. On the ground he had a long AWOL record and in the air he drew a reputation as a headstrong individualist who deserted patrols to go after the enemy. Sometime during his brief career with the 27th Aero Squadron, to which he was assigned, he became obsessed with the idea of knocking observation balloons out of the sky, always a risky business because of the calculated crossfire ground batteries could send up around them. Within just a few weeks at the front — or about 30 total hours of flying time—Luke downed fourteen balloons and four airplanes. On his last flight, when he

Right
Members of the U.S. 11th Bombardment Squadron
at base in France

Below
Famous Allied and German fighter
planes of the 1917-18 period

was under open arrest for refusing to obey orders grounding him, Luke blasted three of the enemy *drachen* from the sky before being nailed himself by a formation of German fighters. Wounded, he managed to set his Spad down in a meadow behind German lines and stumbled into a church graveyard. There he died, refusing to surrender to German infantrymen. Luke would surely have been court-martialled had he returned. Instead he received a Congressional Medal for his courageous act, the only American airman to have that distinction while the war was in progress.

Besides the men in the U.S.A.S., several hundred Americans served with foreign squadrons even after America entered the war. A contingent of Yanks under the command of Major Fiorello LaGuardia flew Caproni bombers on the Italian front. Another group served with the R.A.F. until American squadrons could be equipped to accommodate them. Two of the top American aces, Elliot White Springs and George Vaughn, both flew with British squadrons, winding up the war with 12 and 13 victories respectively. Springs landed in fast company in the R.A.F.'s No. 85 Squadron which boasted such aces as Mickey Mannock and Billy Bishop. He eventually rejoined the Americans as a member of the 148th Squadron and later wrote several books about his colorful flying career. Vaughn was assigned to the British 84th Squadron, with which he downed seven of the enemy before being transferred to the American 17th, where he added six more victories. Another high scorer who served with the R.A.F. was Field Kindley, a one-time Arkansas farmboy who once attacked German infantry and rail transports, shot down an enemy two-seater, forced down a balloon and frightened two Fokkers away from a lone comrade after his ammunition had run out — all within two hours. Kindley

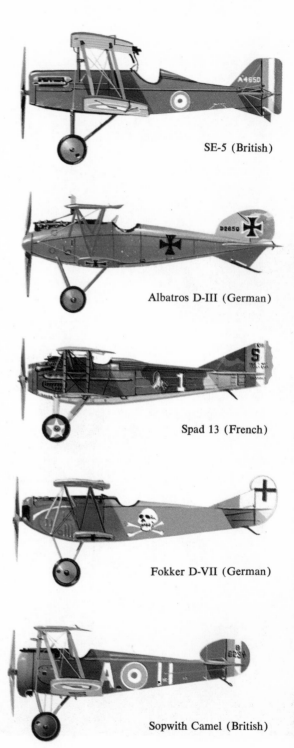

SE-5 (British)

Albatros D-III (German)

Spad 13 (French)

Fokker D-VII (German)

Sopwith Camel (British)

first served with the British 65th Squadron, then with the American 148th where both he and Springs were flight leaders. Kindley scored 12 victories before being killed in combat. Kindley, Vaughn and Springs maintained their British ways in at least one respect after leaving the R.A.F. With the British they had flown the highly respected SE-5 fighter, and with the American units they flew another British-made plane, the Sopwith Camel, tricky to control but also respected for its great maneuverability.

Fighter pilots grabbed most of the glory during the First World War but they were by no means the only airmen to make an important contribution. American observation squadrons, for instance, performed yeoman work, taking 18,000 photographs and logging 35,000 hours over the front, in spite of being hampered by inferior equipment. Many of the observation units flew obsolescent airplanes like the Sopwith 1½ Strutter, the inferior Avion Renault, or the Spad 11, a two-seat version of the famous Spad pursuit ship but a dud as a reconnaissance plane. Eventually most of the Air Service's observation squadrons were standardized with an airplane worthy of their efforts: the Salmson 2A2, a French-built two-seater equipped with self-sealing gas tanks and introducing the radial engine to combat.

One of the great moments in American observation work came, however, in another airplane — the controversial DH-4, British-designed but made in quantity in American factories. A DH-4-equipped observation squadron, No. 50, flew repeatedly into a low ravine during the bitter Argonne battle in search of Major Charles Whittlesey's "Lost Battalion." So deep did the Yank pilots fly that German machine guns were actually directing a withering fire at them from the heights above. Two of the 50th Squadron's airmen, Harold Goettler and Erwin Bleckley,

received posthumous Congressional Medals for their attempts to aid the stray unit.

Another remarkable observation flight was performed by the combat commander of Air Service himself, Colonel William "Billy" Mitchell. During July 1918 the French and Americans knew a big new German attack would be launched along the Marne but could not determine at which points the enemy would cross the river. Mitchell, without waiting for a second-hand report, took up a Spad himself and followed the Marne upstream. He passed several Fokkers as he peered below, but they either did not see him or paid no attention to him. Then, near Dormans, he spotted large concentrations of enemy troops crossing the river on pontoon bridges. They were without air support and apparently oblivious to his Spad's presence. Mitchell banked for home to order an immediate air strike.

"Looking down on the men, marching so splendidly," he wrote later, "I thought to myself, what a shame to spoil such fine infantry."

American bombing squadrons worked courageously but, like observation units, they lacked first-class airplanes. Vaunted Handley-Page bombers from Britain never materialized. French Breguet bombers were preferred by the American units but the Yank

Gen. "Billy" Mitchell (right) and Gen. Mason Patrick

55

flyers often had to make do with Salmsons and DH-4's improvised as bombers. Neither was capable of carrying more than a few light bombs.

Bomber flying could be extremely hazardous work, especially when fighter escorts were missing. One such unaccompanied flight of 18 bombing planes returned from a mission during the American squeeze on the St. Mihiel salient in September with only five of its planes left. One squadron, the 11th, was nearly knocked permanently out of action on its second day of operations when only one riddled airplane out of a flight of six returned from a melee with a large swarm of enemy fighters. The 11th was temporarily withdrawn from action until it could be re-equipped with new Breguets.

World War I bombing raids were dwarf-sized by comparison with some of the huge raids of World War II. The figures rolled up in the First War's biggest bombing raid on October 9, 1918, however, look reasonably impressive even beside the standards of the later conflict. Participating were American, French and British airmen, who combined in an attempt to smash German troop concentrations and supplies during the Battle of the Argonne. Allied ground troops were awed to look up and see 322 airplanes fill the skies above; together the planes dumped 39 tons of bombs. That same night British flyers dropped 41 tons more on supply points, making a total of 80 tons unloaded in one day.

Really effective bombardment — the concept of strategic bombing — had to wait until a new era in military thinking. Ground generals still dominated the Air Service and its Allied counterparts during World War I, and infantry leaders wanted air action that would directly benefit their foot soldiers, nothing more. Men like Billy Mitchell and British General Sir Hugh ("Boom") Trenchard advocated long-range strategic air

strikes but their views were not put into practice for nearly 25 years.

The role of the fighter airplane emerged more clearly. Without control of the skies, it was learned, control of the ground was impossible — and such control could only be achieved with the pursuit plane. For the fighter there evolved a sophisticated set of tactics and a variety of different duties, which included not only the celebrated dogfight but strafing, escort work and even light bombing raids. Yet advancing technology kept rewriting the rules in fighter flying. Today's hot new plane could become tomorrow's cast-off; armaments changed and some tactics taught during the war were discarded as weaponry and aircraft progressed.

The air war of 1914-1918 was unique. It was a starting point and it established the first rules. But it was never again duplicated. The air war remains a vivid moment in history because it was a pioneering effort, charted with bravery and skill by the airmen who participated in it.

9
Too Little and Too Late

While the U.S. Air Service strove to become an effective fighting instrument on the Western Front, American industry was having its own struggles at home. Renowned for its role in revolutionizing the automobile industry, American manufacturing seemed the potential savior to the supply problems that had plagued Allied air services. Prophecies that the United States would "darken the skies of Europe" were heard across the land. A joint Army-Navy technical team mapped a starry-eyed program calling for 22,625 planes and 45,000 engines. Congress proved itself eager to provide the means for a huge air program by appropriating $640 million for aircraft production and training three months after the nation entered the war — the largest sum ever approved for a single purpose up to that time.

The performance, unfortunately, never lived up to the promise. Massive waves of airplanes boasted by some authorities in the United States never materialized. After months of delay, deliveries did begin in substantial quantities, but not all the aircraft delivered could be flown immediately. Of 1,200 combat aircraft which had reached France by November 11, 1918, only 196 found their way into American squadrons. The remainder were in various stages of preparation for combat, in training use, or were unfit for combat duty. Even more disappointing to the mightiest industrial nation in the world was the fact that, except for a small number of Curtiss flying boats in service off coastal waters, not one American design had entered the fight. American flyers manned Spads, Camels, Nieuports and other foreign models while engineers at home still labored to turn their designs from blueprint to reality. The one combat airplane produced in quantity in America was not even a native design; it was the British De Havilland 4, an effective two-seat observation plane when introduced

to the front in 1917, but already obsolescent when the Armistice was signed.

Why did industry fail? As the answers emerged in congressional hearings and public statements after the war, they drew a picture of confusion and indecision coupled with a number of genuine handicaps to production. There was some evidence, for instance, that British and French manufacturers had made their technological information hard to obtain early in the war out of their fear of American competition. Once the United States entered the war, air leaders vacillated over the best designs; the public would take pride in a home-grown product, but many technicians recognized their Allies' lead in aircraft design and production and decided to concentrate on proven foreign models.

Moreover, military aviation in America was in such a pitiful state of unpreparedness in April 1917, that even an industrial complex well-oiled and ready to go would have had a hard time living up to expectations in the short period allotted to it. What steps had been taken to organize an aerial force were largely the result of the Army's experience on the Mexican border the year before, when the Signal Corps had suffered through lack of funds, too few men and Curtiss Jennies ill-equipped for the rigors of the American southwest. Congress had awakened after that with an appropriation of $13 million for aviation purposes, but military brass hats still seemed curiously blind to the importance of putting muscle into its air arm. When America enlisted in the European war not one combat plane was owned by the United States Army. It had only two flying fields and a small number of training planes, none of which was up to date. The Army — and the industrial complex behind it — was practically starting from scratch in building an air force.

Within weeks after its entry in the war, the United States learned the scope of the air-

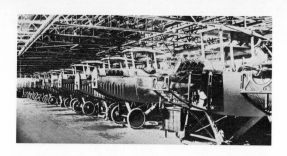

craft problem when French Premier Alexandre Ribot cabled President Wilson that thousands of planes, pilots and mechanics would be needed at the front by the following spring. (Ribot's actual figures were 4,500 planes, 5,000 pilots and 50,000 mechanics, with enough additional manpower and supplies to "enable the Allies to win supremacy of the air.") As a result a team of Army and Navy air officials under Major Benjamin Foulois (the former Mexican border air commander was by this time senior flying officer in Washington) drew up an ambitious program calling for a combat force of 12,000 aircraft, 45,000 engines and, in addition, thousands more of training craft. Congress made the money available during July but a decision had yet to be made on the kind of planes to be produced. Out of a welter of confusion in Washington came the appointment of a special commission to select aircraft headed by Major Raynal C. Bolling, a longtime aviation enthusiast and former general counsel to the United States Steel Corporation. By midsummer, the Bolling Commission reported back that aircraft were needed primarily for (1) training, (2) close support or tactical cooperation with ground troops, and (3) strategic or offensive missions against the enemy. More specifically, it chose four aircraft as suitable for production in the United States: the DH-4 and Bristol F2B, both British designs; the French Spad 13 pursuit ship, and the Italian Caproni bomber.

Of the Bolling Commission's four recommended designs, only the DH-4 would ever reach the front. Indecision and delay clouded planning for other types, the example of the Spad being typical. A sample of the fighter, among the most highly touted of all Allied "chasse" planes, was shipped to America in September 1917, where it was intended for conversion to the new American-built Liberty engine. It was soon apparent, however, that

the big Liberty could not be adapted to the Spad's snub-nosed frame. Cables from the U.S. Air Service in France, meanwhile, indicated that the production of fighter aircraft might best be left to the Allies, and so contracts with the Curtiss company for 3,000 Spads were cancelled. Five months later, American Expeditionary Force leaders on the battle scene witnessed a growing shortage of single-seat fighters and advised the immediate production of this type in America. This time the Curtiss factory received a contract for SE-5's and went through the complex process of planning and tooling up for mass production of the British-designed fighter. The results were not surprising. Of 1,000 SE-5's contracted for, only one was produced before the Armistice — and that one was equipped with a 180-horsepower engine — while the British were by this time installing engines of 210 horsepower in their own SE-5's.

Attempts to produce the Bristol F2B, a British two-seater of sterling qualities, proved even more inept. A fast, high-flying airplane which was so good it remained in active RAF service until 1932, the Bristol was fitted with a Liberty engine in America and prepared for tests. Each one taken up crashed. In July 1918, the contract with Curtiss for 2,000 Bristols was cancelled after the expenditure of more than $6 million.

The production of bombers ran into the same obstacles of delay, indecision and confusion as those faced in making pursuit types. The Bolling mission had chosen the Caproni bomber as desirable, but others in America leaned toward the Handley-Page 0/400 twin-engine bomber, a British design on which rested hopes for massive bombing of Germany. When production of the Caproni became bogged down in the confusion of converting Italian-language plans to English and meeting stiff Italian design specifications, American military authorities turned to the Handley-

U.S. aircraft production program was built
around the famous Liberty engine.
The Liberty "Twelve" proved to be a fine motor
but too heavy for light, fast combat planes
needed in Europe

Page. But production of the British plane also dragged. By war's end not one aircraft of either model had been readied for front-line duty.

The record of the DH-4's was more impressive in terms of numbers of airplanes produced but it was riddled with arguments over the merits of the model. The De Havilland's top speed of 117 m.p.h., its ceiling of 16,000 feet and its general effectiveness as an observation aircraft and day bomber were rapidly being outclassed by similar enemy types as the war entered its final phases. Nevertheless, American manufacturers went ahead with mass production of the model and by the Armistice had turned out nearly 5,000 machines, 1,200 of which were shipped overseas. Those that crossed the Atlantic eventually equipped five bombing and seven observation squadrons of the U.S. Air Service.

The significant number of DH-4's produced in a comparatively short period of time (they were ordered into production on October 18, 1917) was offset by their performance in the air. The 400-plus horsepower Liberty engine adapted to its frame as a replacement for its original Rolls-Royce power plant was substituted at the cost of the life of Major Oscar Brindley, one of the nation's top test pilots who died putting the plane and its new engine through rigorous trials over Dayton, Ohio. When it went into combat, the DH-4 remained controversial even among those who flew it. Because its gas tank was placed in a vulnerable position between pilot and observer, it was dubbed the "Flaming Coffin," although its loss rate was not greater than other two-seaters at the close of the war. Some pilots complained that poor visibility from the cockpit made close formation flying impossible, others that the distance between pilot and observer made communication difficult. Still others, though, praised it as the best two-seater at the front. Captain Daniel P. Morse, commander of the 50th Aero Squadron, said it was especially effective at low altitudes where the American squadrons did most of their flying, and that it could outdistance and outclimb anything the Germans had.

Criticism of the DH-4 did not stop with the end of the war. Some engineers insisted that a modified version of the 4, the DH-9, was a better airplane but that American industry had built the 4 out of expedience. The DH-9 was actually as controversial a plane in Britain as the DH-4 was in America, owing

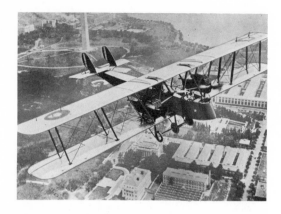

mainly to the unreliability of its BHP (Beardmore-Halford-Pullinger) engine. Eventually 14,000 American-built 9's were ordered but only a dozen of the planes were completed before the war ended.

Despite its failure to turn out the waves of combat airplanes expected of it, American industry scored significant successes in two other facets of aircraft production. One was the development of an outstanding engine, the Liberty, and the other was the mass production of that durable trainer, the Curtiss JN-4. In one other area, too, it made a significant contribution with a flying boat which set design standards for years following.

The Liberty engine was one of the first problems tackled by wartime industry. American air leaders, determining that the profusion of Allied engine types were creating an enormous parts and replacements headache, decided to make a fresh start by building their own engine. Such an engine would have to be considerably more powerful than existing models in order to stay ahead of rapid technical advances, yet be simple enough for mass production. Two engine experts, Elbert J. Hall and Jesse G. Vincent, went to work behind closed doors in a Washington hotel suite and within 48 hours emerged with the basic design of the Liberty. A little over a month later, on July 3, 1917, the first

Liberty, an eight-cylinder model, was tested; during August a more powerful 12-cylinder version underwent tests. By the end of the year seven automobile manufacturers were turning out the new engine. By the time the war had ended almost a year later more than 13,500 Libertys had been produced.

The Liberty was both powerful for its time and, after its shakedown period, solidly reliable. The basic 12-cylinder model, a V-type, developed 400 horsepower and had a weight of 1.8 pounds per horsepower, a full pound lighter than rival power plants. The Liberty also proved itself easily adaptable to change. The first model developed 330 horsepower but as revamped in later models it could turn out 440 horsepower. In fact, the Liberty was such a good engine it has been accused of holding back the development of aircraft after the war, for thousands of surplus Libertys went on being used in various civil aircraft during the 1920's.

In the production of airframes, American industry made its greatest contribution with training planes. Taking its cue from the Bolling Mission's emphasis on the importance of such airplanes, it launched right into full-scale production of the Curtiss JN-4. By the end of the war more than 5,500 of the popular "Jennies" had been produced. Industry had, with this ubiquitous two-seater, a thoroughly tested design which continually underwent refinements as the war progressed. A variety of Jennies were made, including the primary trainer-type powered with the OX-5, a 90-horsepower engine; an advanced trainer equipped with a 150-horsepower Hispano-Suiza; and a seaplane version, the N-9, packing a slightly more powerful OX-6 engine rated at 100 horsepower. So durable were Jennies that they stayed around for many years after the war, becoming the standard barnstorming plane during the 1920's and continuing in use by the Air Corps until 1927.

The single-seat Thomas Morse MB-3
became the standard Army
fighter in the 1920's

Still another home-grown product scored a miniature triumph in May 1917 by knocking out a German U-boat and a Zeppelin within the period of a week. The plane was the Curtiss H-12, a twin-engine flying boat whose prototype was the *America* flying boat which Glenn Curtiss had hoped would be the first to fly across the Atlantic. The outbreak of the war had spoiled that plan, but the British saw practical possibilities in the plane and purchased more than 50 during 1914 and 1915. Near duplicates of the *America,* they were designated Curtiss H-4. Later versions added both size and power, and it was in one of these so-called "Large Americas" that British flyers gunned down a German dirigible over the North Sea on May 14, 1917. Six days later another British-flown H-12 became the first plane to sink a U-boat. The H-12's acquired an unfortunate reputation for unseaworthiness and were succeeded by the H-16, an improved model with a redesigned hull and either Rolls-Royce or Liberty engines. U.S. Navy patrols flew them in 1918 and although they never managed to sink a submarine, they kept the German undersea raiders on the run.

If the war had gone into 1919 the United States would have had a number of its own airplanes in action. As the war ended at least four combat-worthy models were in the making. One of these, the Packard-Le Père LUSAC-11, was shipped to France and was undergoing tests when the war came to an abrupt end. Trials showed that this sturdy two-seater was maneuverable and fast, with a top speed of 133 miles an hour. It also was the first American production airplane to be equipped with a supercharged engine (a 425-horsepower Liberty), which gave it a service ceiling of over 20,000 feet. Another two-seater to begin tests late in 1918 was the Loening M-8, a high-wing monoplane equipped with a 300-horsepower Wright-Hispano engine capable of 143.5 miles an hour. Like the Packard-Le Père it was scheduled for mass producton but the war's end halted orders. Early in 1919 another American fighter, the single-seat Thomas-Morse MB-3, made its first flight. The "Tommy Morse" could do 152 miles an hour and became the standard Army fighter during the early 1920's. It carried a 300-horsepower Wright H engine and in late versions fitted a belly fuel tank which extended its range to 400 miles.

Other native designs to make their appearance just after the war ended included the Orenco D single engine fighter, a Spad-like model designed by Army engineers, and the Curtiss 18 "Kirkham" two-seater which was available in either triplane or biplane models. The "tripe" version set a new U.S. altitude record of 32,450 feet in August 1919.

A serviceable American bomber would have been ready for combat, too, if the war had lasted into 1919. It was the Martin MB-1, a four-place, twin-engine biplane for which Glenn Martin received an Army contract early in 1918. The MB-1 was officially designated as a reconnaissance plane, but it could carry 1,040 pounds of bombs and bristled with five .30 caliber machine guns. Only nine planes were built before the Armistice.

Peace quickly took the thrust out of the development of military airplanes. The Army, rather than planning on new and better aircraft, was faced with the big task of dumping thousands of useless airplanes as war surplus. Besides, hadn't the fight just fought been "the war to end wars"? With this in mind, advances in aerial warfare would seem absurd in a warless world.

So went the thinking of a joyous America welcoming its boys back home. The time had come to renew peaceful pursuits; the war was over and ahead lay a whole world to conquer. Aviation now made ready to meet new challenges unrelated to war.

10
Across the Atlantic

In the spring of 1919, a war-weary world turned away from the horrors of conflict and looked toward more constructive deeds. The world of aviation was astir with new hopes and new challenges. During the war, airplanes had made enormous strides under the rigorous demands of aerial combat. Speeds had reached nearly 150 miles per hour in fast pursuit planes being built as the Armistice was announced in November 1918. The British had developed a huge four-engine Handley-Page bomber designed to drop its bombs on Berlin and return to Allied territory. Although it never saw action, this and other aircraft like it opened the eyes of aviation men to the new possibilities for long-range flight.

Of all the high hurdles still to be jumped, the Atlantic Ocean offered the greatest immediate rewards. Not only would its great distance and fierce weather conditions prove a true test of men and machines, but its conquest would surely pave the way for a regular transatlantic air route that would bring two continents within hours of each other. Airmen had long dreamed of conquering the Atlantic. The American Prof. Thaddeus Lowe, as early as 1860, had started out in a balloon from Ohio but never got near the water. The journalist, Walter Wellman, attempted an Atlantic crossing in 1910 in his dirigible *America* but came down 400 miles out at sea, drifting helplessly with the wind after an engine failed.

The end of World War I came as a signal for aviators to try their hand at an Atlantic crossing. Besides the honor of being first across, a fresh incentive had been added. In 1913, Lord Northcliffe, publisher of the London *Daily Mail,* had offered a prize of $50,000 to the first airmen to fly nonstop across the Atlantic. Early in 1919 the newspaper renewed the offer. With this substantial reward in the offing, several British aircraft companies and flyers began making prepara-

tions for the attempt. Of nine separate possibilities in Great Britain, three teams of airmen, each of them led by seasoned pilots, emerged as the leading contenders to make the first Atlantic crossing.

In America, the U.S. Navy was eyeing the Atlantic as a prize that would surely win glory for its own name and for the nation. The Navy's fledgling aviation arm was certain it had the aircraft that could do the job in its recently designed NC flying boat, built as a joint venture with Glenn Curtiss' plant in Buffalo, N.Y. ("NC" stood for "Navy-Curtiss"). This unwieldy looking plane, conceived near the end of the war to fly the Atlantic and hunt submarines off the British coast, was powered by four 400-horsepower Liberty engines mounted between biplane wings. The "Nancies," as the NC's were soon called, were among the largest planes of their day, with a 126-foot wingspread and a weight of more than 28,000 pounds fully loaded. Navy and Curtiss engineers under the supervision of G. C. Westervelt had worked hard to get the right hull, light yet durable enough to withstand the pounding of seas in case of a dunking. They settled on a 45-foot, pod-like hull with the tail extending aft on three hollow wooden booms and engines riding between the two wings in a maze of struts and wires. Glenn Curtiss, himself a master designer, had doubts about the NC blueprints.

Although they both aimed to be first across the ocean, the Americans and the British had somewhat different objectives. The three contending British biplanes, equipped only with landing gear, had sufficient ranges to make a nonstop flight over the North Atlantic if the most advantageous route was charted. The Americans, despite the ability of the NC's to land on water and the power generated by their big Liberty engines, had found during tests that the great weight of "Nancies" prevented them from carrying enough fuel to

One of the largest planes of its day, the four-engined Navy Curtiss seaplane was designed for possible Atlantic crossing

make a nonstop trip. The Navy therefore mapped a multi-legged trip, picking the Azores in mid-ocean as a refueling point that could carry them on to the continent. Thus ineligible for the $50,000 non-stop prize, the Navy declared it would send three NC's across purely for scientific purposes.

A watching world knew better. The breaking of the transatlantic barrier — money or no money — would be a giant feather in the cap of the nation and the airmen who accomplished it. As May 1919 approached, the British and the Americans began converging on Newfoundland for the assault on the Atlantic. Prevailing winds dictated that a west-to-east attempt would be the most practical; the bleak island of Newfoundland, jutting into the Atlantic toward Europe, became the logical jumping-off point.

The three NC's groomed for the American flight were placed under the overall command of one of the Navy's most illustrious flyers, Commander John H. Towers. A former pupil of Curtiss, Towers had earned his aviator's license in 1911 and a year later had set the world's endurance record for hydroplanes. Towers was to man the flagship NC-3 while Lieutenant Commander Patrick N. L. ("Pat") Bellinger was at the helm of the NC-1. Lieutenant Commander Albert C. Read, less

63

Crew of the NC-4 with Commander Read at the far right

well known in aviation circles than Towers or Bellinger, was to command the third flying boat, the NC-4. The NC-2 was missing from the roster since it had been dismantled to provide parts for the other three flying boats.

Of all the airmen preparing that spring to pioneer an Atlantic hop, "Putty" Read seemed the least likely to succeed. He had received his Navy wings only four years earlier, and had sat out America's part in World War I by directing routine flights off Long Island shores. A quiet, reserved New Englander who rarely smiled, Read had acquired his nickname because of the immobility of his features. Only five-foot-four, he looked more like a racehorse jockey than an aviator. Yet, within a month Putty Read would be a hero, making headlines in every daily newspaper in the United States, and decorated by a President. One popular magazine of the era tagged him with a name that seemed to fit perfectly: "The Christopher Columbus of Aviation."

The start of the great Navy flight was almost disastrous for Read, his NC-4 and his crew of five men. The three flying boats had left Rockaway, Long Island, in good order on May 8, bound for Newfoundland. Off Cape Cod the NC-4 threw a connecting rod in one engine and developed faulty oil pressure in another. Read had to bring her down 80 miles from the coast and taxi through the night to reach the Chatham, Mass., Naval Station. Six days passed before repairs could be made and weather was clear enough for the plane to continue. Nevertheless, Read was reasonably confident as he left Chatham on May 14th that he could catch up with Towers and Bellinger, who were socked in themselves by continuing poor weather in Newfoundland. Halfway there, Read's plane came down again with engine trouble, this time in Halifax, Nova Scotia. While the little commander and his men

chafed, sailors taunted them with jibes about their "hoodoo" plane, and their "lame duck." The next day the NC-4 resumed its flight to Newfoundland, desperately fighting against time. Would Towers decide to leave without him, thereby completely eliminating him from the race? As an anguished Read approached the Newfoundland base through breaking clouds, Bellinger's "One" and Towers' "Three" were plowing through the water in a sprint for takeoff. Read's dismay turned to joy moments later as he saw his sister boats refuse to lift. As Read landed, the two discouraged commanders steered their planes back to a naval supply ship anchored in the bay.

It was determined that by gassing up while on the water, the NC's 1 and 3 had taken on an extra 200 pounds of fuel. Now they drained off the excess (and grounded one protesting crew member from Towers' craft to further lighten the load), and with an overnight layover to allow Read time for last-minute preparations, all three boats charged up the bay and rose slowly into the air. Except for a few scary moments as Bellinger struggled for altitude, the Navy planes were up in good shape. Before them, all the way to the Azores, stretched a line of 25 destroyers spaced 50 miles apart as guideposts. As night fell the sister planes watched the stars above and the bursting star shells from the destroyers below. Read, settled in his open cockpit forward, his charts and navigation instruments nearby within the hull, listened with satisfaction to the smoothly purring Libertys.

The "One" and the "Three," however, soon had problems. Bellinger's craft was fighting a bad right torque, evidently the result of a wing replacement back in Long Island. Co-pilot Lou Barin and Pilot Marc Mitscher — the same Mitscher who was to become a World War II Navy hero in the Pacific — labored to keep the plane steady. Towers' flagship was having radio difficulty,

and when darkness closed in he discovered the "Three's" running lights were not working. At one point it narrowly missed a collision with Bellinger's plane. After that Towers ordered each "Nancy" to fly on alone without trying to maintain contact.

Putty Read's "lame duck" flew into the dawn with everything working perfectly, as he later reported. The crew broke out sandwiches, thermos-bottled coffee and chocolate candy. Ensign Herbert C. Rodd, the radioman, sent a message to his mother via a coastal station 750 miles away. But soon after dawn a dense fog formed and Read and his men lost all sense of direction, a problem which was to plague all the early Atlantic flights. Suddenly the commander noticed his compass rotating crazily before him. The NC-4 was falling into a steep bank and was on the verge of going into a fatal nosedive. Read, seated forward, waved wildly at co-pilot Elmer Stone at the controls. At first Stone didn't see, then realized what was happening. The NC-4 leveled off.

Miles away, Towers and Bellinger were groping through the overcast trying to fix their positions. Before the flight began a brilliant young Navy lieutenant commander, Richard E. Byrd, had given each of the NC's two instruments he had recently invented to aid aerial navigation: a wind-and-drift indicator and an aerial sextant. Under nearly blind-flying conditions, they became practically useless. Almost simultaneously, without realizing it, Towers and Bellinger decided to make ocean landings to get their bearings. It was a costly mistake for both of them. The NC-1 tore into a huge wavecrest and emerged with sagging wings, a broken tail and a badly leaking hull. Bellinger calculated his position at about 100 miles west of the Azores and began sending out a weak SOS. Towers, like Bellinger, looked at the ocean below and believed a landing would not be too risky.

Down close, he saw too late that seas were running heavy. The NC-3 bounced off one comber, topped another and spun into a deep trough. Water poured into the hull; struts and wires dangled out of kilter; one engine sagged between the wings.

Read flew on alone now, keeping in touch with the destroyers with the aid of his radio. Weather was still terrible, but surprisingly he had made better time than the NC-1 and NC-3. By midday he peered through a break in the clouds and spotted a tide rip in the water, an almost sure sign that land was near. Two minutes later he and the crew made out a rocky shoreline — the tip of Flores Island, westernmost of the Azores. "It was the most welcome sight we had even seen," the commander of the "Four" later wrote.

Keeping low in the murk, the NC-4 headed for the near port of Horta in the Azores. It actually put down first in a deserted bay and had to take off again. Six minutes later it touched down off Horta and taxied toward the destroyer *Columbia*.

Meanwhile, Towers and his men, drenched and fearful that the NC-3 would capsize, received the news of Read's landing at Horta but were unable to reply due to a damaged

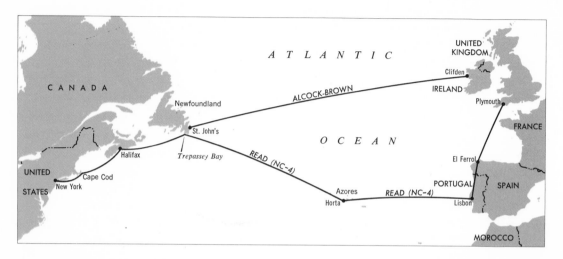

transmitter. They also heard an all-out search was being made for them — 100 miles away. And they heard that Bellinger and his NC-1 crew had been picked up by a Greek freighter, *Ionia,* that had wandered into their view. The freighter, it turned out, couldn't have heard Bellinger's SOS in any event: it had no radio. That left the NC-3 on the water alone, in grave danger. A gale with winds up to 60 miles per hour whipped up big waves that rolled the plane threateningly. Some of the crew were seasick. A wing pontoon tore off, requiring one crewman to sit on the opposite wingtip to keep the plane from flipping over. Food was soaked; the only water they were able to drink came from engine radiators.

On the second day adrift Towers and his men sighted land. A destroyer steamed out to rescue them but Towers insisted on making their way in alone. Half drifting and half with the help of battered engines they made their way slowly into harbor. It was Ponta Delgada, the Azores port to which they had originally intended to fly. The ordeal of the NC-3 was destined to have nearly as much impact on world opinion as Read's successful flight. Towers' flying boat had traveled 205 miles in 60 hours, drifting backwards most of the

way. It showed that the sea could be a safety cushion for overseas flights provided they used the right planes and equipment.

Back in Newfoundland, the Englishmen heard of Read's arrival in the Azores and knew they had to take off immediately to capture the Atlantic glory. With Read delayed anew by weather in the Azores, they knew that their faster planes still could beat the Americans to the other side.

First off was a team manned by the colorful Harry G. Hawker and his co-pilot K. MacKenzie Grieve. Although the weather was foul over the North Atlantic that May 16th, they hoisted their Sopwith biplane *Atlantic* off the runway and headed out over storm-tossed seas. Everything went well at first, until Hawker noticed the temperature gauge rising. Its engine ready to quit at any moment, the *Atlantic* ditched near a Danish freighter, which went to the flyers' rescue.

Shortly after the departure of Hawker and Grieve, another two-man team made up of the veteran airman Frederick P. Raynham and his navigator Capt. William Morgan strapped themselves into the cockpit of their Martynside biplane *Raymor* (a combination of the airmen's names) and rumbled over

British flyers, John Alcock and Arthur Brown, made the first nonstop flight across the Atlantic

their primitive runway. A crosswind caught the heavily loaded plane and dumped it head first into the turf. Damage was too great for another immediate attempt.

The failure of the first two British flights took the pressure off Read and his NC-4 crew for the time being. They still had a crucial lap to Portugal before them, but it was reported that the third British plane, to be flown by John Alcock and his navigator, Arthur W. Brown, would not be ready for another month. By May 27th the weather had brightened in the Azores and the "Four" roared off toward the continent. Nine hours and 43 minutes later it landed in Lisbon, where the populace went wild.

"U.S. Airmen First To Cross Atlantic," said banner headlines in the New York *Herald*. "NC-4 Wins First Ocean Flight For America," said *The New York Times*. President Woodrow Wilson, who was then in Paris for peace talks, wired Read: "We are heartily proud of you. You have won the distinction of adding further laurels to our country."

One more leg was left, a final jump to Plymouth, England, which was chosen as the last stop because its American namesake had meant a safe landing for a band of Atlantic pioneers nearly 300 years earlier. Now in a jaunty mood, Putty Read delighted newsreel men who had missed his Lisbon arrival by repeating the historic landing for the benefit of their grinding cameras. Then he soared off again bound for England. Minor engine trouble forced the NC-4 down again briefly along the Spanish coast, but on May 31st it appeared in the gray skies over Plymouth, where it thrilled a large crowd assembled on the shore by banking, circling and sailing in for a landing.

The English had been robbed of a conquest of the Atlantic themselves but now gave their hearts to the Americans. Read was hoisted above shoulders in Plymouth streets,

then went on to London for a tumultuous reception in the British capital. The Prince of Wales greeted the airmen, as did Winston Churchill. A new ovation was given to them in Paris, where President Wilson decorated the pint-sized NC-4 leader with the Distinguished Flying Medal.

Two weeks after the Americans arrived in England, Alcock and Brown took off from Newfoundland in their converted twin-engine Vickers "Vimy" bomber. After 16 hours and 28 minutes of flight they landed safely — although a little embarrassingly — in an Irish bog. Alcock and Brown went on to receive the accolades of their countrymen and the *Daily Mail's* $50,000 for the first nonstop Atlantic crossing.

The NC-4's epic flight faded into obscurity in the next few years as new names challenged the Atlantic. Two months after Read's achievement the British dirigible R-34 created a sensation by crossing the ocean both ways. Soon after the turn of the 1920's airmen began shooting for new nonstop records. A number of tragedies and a few glittering successes were the result. Among the heartbreaking failures was the France-to-America attempt of the French war hero Charles Nungesser and his partner François Coli. Among those who were successful were Charles A. Lindbergh, and later in 1927, Richard E. Byrd and Clarence Chamberlin.

It was many years before attention returned to Read and the NC-4 flight. After World War II, the National Air Museum of the Smithsonian Institution collected parts from the "Four," gathering dust in obscure shops and flying fields along the East Coast, and assembled them for display in Washington, D.C.

For a long time Commander Read lived in retirement across the Potomac not far from his NC-4. He died in relative obscurity in October 1967. His place in aviation history, however, is secure.

11
Record Makers

The first Atlantic crossing whetted flyers' appetites for new record-making flights. Airmen were a naturally adventurous breed, but coupled with their venturesome spirit was the sincere desire of many to advance the cause of aviation. Aware that public interest in air progress had slackened after World War I, they knew also that the public was thrilled by the news of a daring flight. The benefits of such an event were quickly apparent. The individual airman could reap the reward of prize money, or if that were lacking, cash in later on his new fame. For the nation's military air arms, a stirring flight could mean sorely needed appropriations from Congress.

Airmen yearned to make new records and cross new distances even when material gains were not in the offing. Like the explorers before them who had dared to venture into uncharted regions, and the spacemen after them who hurtled beyond the earth's atmosphere, the aviators of the Twenties were driven by Man's indomitable desire to find new paths into the unknown . . . to conquer the unconquerable.

A succession of long-range hops followed the first transatlantic flights. In addition to the Navy's Atlantic crossing, and that of Alcock and Brown, the year 1919 saw two other long-distance jumps, one by the Australians, Ross and Keith Smith, along an 11,000-mile route from England to Australia, and the other by four U.S. Army flyers who took a Martin bomber "Round the Rim" of the United States, covering 9,823 miles in 78 days. The same year, the British dirigible R-34 floated across the Atlantic — and back — with an ease that made lighter-than-air craft look like an ideal aerial vehicle for long-range flights. In 1920 another U.S. Army team flew from New York to Alaska, and in 1921 a new transcontinental airmail relay record of 33 hours began to shrink the breadth of the American continent to manageable proportions.

By 1922 two American airmen were ready to take on another big one — a transcontinental, nonstop trip across America. A flight across the continent posed as many problems in its own way as an Atlantic crossing, for across this vast stretch of land lay both the imposing mountains of the Appalachian range, and the more formidable heights of the Rockies. A hop across America would push an aviator both far and high. Supporting the project from the start was Brigadier General William Mitchell, the redoubtable air combat commander of war fame who now dominated the peacetime U.S. Air Service. Endowed with a shrewd eye for publicity, Mitchell knew a crosscountry flight could give the Air Service enormous prestige. Eager to make the attempt were two tough, experienced Air Service test pilots, Lieutenants Oakley Kelly, who had suggested the flight in the first place, and John Macready, a former boxer, cattleman and lawyer who had established a world's altitude record of more than 40,000 feet in 1921. A series of disappointments and near disasters lay ahead of this hardy pair of flyers, but in the end they won the victory they sought.

A transcontinental nonstop flight would have been impossible with the equipment the Air Service had on hand early in 1922. In June of that year, though, it purchased two large monoplanes from the Dutch aerial genius, Anthony Fokker. One of them was given exhaustive tests under the scrutiny of Kelly and a crack engineer, Lieutenant Ernest Dichman, and was determined capable of making the long journey. Fokker's T-2, as it was designated, wasn't a very graceful bird even by 1922 standards. Its boxy fuselage began with a fat, squatty nose and ended with a shriveled fin atop the fuselage. Close to the nose was placed a wide wing with a span of 79 feet 6 inches, built more for the lift it

The first nonstop flight across the United
States was made by Army service pilots in
a Fokker T-2 monoplane

could provide than for beauty. Power was
supplied by a 420-horsepower Liberty engine,
and fuel was stored in two wing tanks plus a
smaller tank installed within the fuselage.
The placement of the pilot was awkward to
say the least: he sat up front in an open cockpit with the big Liberty as his right-hand
companion and the leading edge of the wing
as his headrest. Tricky timing was required
for a switch of positions between pilot and
relief pilot. On receiving a signal from the
man at the controls, the airman inside the
fuselage took over on a set of duplicate
controls placed in an interior position having
only limited visibility through side windows
and no view forward. While the plane was
thus being flown nearly blind, the pilot slipped
back and took over the interior controls,
after which his replacement crawled forward
and squeezed into the cockpit.

Early on October 5, 1922, Kelly and
Macready climbed aboard the glistening dark
blue T-2 at Rockwell Field in San Diego and
revved the Liberty. Having decided on a
west-to-east flight to take advantage of prevailing tailwinds, the pilots knew at the same
time that they would be faced with hurdling
the Rockies before enough fuel had burned
off to make the heavily loaded plane signi-
ficantly lighter. Inside the T-2 sandwiches,
coffee and soup were stowed away to sustain
the pilots over their grueling course. Outside,
a small crowd of well-wishers shouted and
waved as the plane rolled down the field.
With Kelly at the controls, the T-2 rose
heavily from the ground and struggled to
gain altitude, dipping dangerously close to the
Pacific Ocean before banking toward the east.
Fifty miles from the field the plane had risen
only 1,700 feet and ahead lay the foothills of
its first mountain range. Instead of trying to
jump the hills, however, Kelly and Macready
turned away, faced with an impenetrable
shroud of fog. Macready later admitted that

the two flyers not only felt it would be suicide to attempt passing over the mountains, but that the course they were now about to follow would save them a lot of embarrassment back in San Diego where a crowd had just given them a royal sendoff. Rather than return immediately to the field, they decided to attempt a new endurance record, and plotted a course up and down the West Coast. After 35 hours and 18 minutes of this monotony, they landed. Their time easily broke the existing record, but it could not be officially recorded because the required sealed barograph was not aboard the Fokker.

Undeterred, Kelly and Macready made ready for another continental crossing, and on November 3 the weather looked good from San Diego clear across the nation. Kelly again took the controls and once more the overloaded T-2 heaved reluctantly into the air. This time skies were crystal clear and the airplane negotiated its previous obstacles with little difficulty. But harrowing moments lay ahead. Some 400 miles out of San Diego Kelly spied water seeping from a hairline crack in the Liberty but he decided that it wasn't serious enough to keep them from reaching New York. Then, over high peaks near Tucson, Arizona, the air became extremely turbulent, and Kelly and Macready held their breath as they headed for what appeared certain collision with the mountains. However, they were swept clear by updrafts just before the moment of impact. Past the peaks, the T-2 flew on over salt flats, still bucking the rough air. As night fell the plane climbed higher, its fuel load decreasing with every mile. Now new turbulence struck as the T-2 winged its way along the fringes of a midwest tornado. Macready fought to control the plane, finally allowing Kelly to take over as the big Fokker approached St. Louis. Just when the weather was clearing, Kelly noticed water streaming from both sides of the Liberty, a sign that the damage spotted earlier was worsening. With Macready once again at the helm, Kelly poured every liquid available, including their remaining soup and coffee, into the engine to keep it from seizing with heat. They set the T-2 down on the parade ground of an Army base near Indianapolis just as the Liberty stopped dead.

The pilots' discouragement at the thought of making a third attempt lasted just 48 hours. Macready and Kelly decided to try again, but with one important difference from the first two efforts. This time they would fly an east-to-west route to take advantage of a lightened fuel load over the Rockies. Accordingly, on May 2, 1923, the Fokker, fitted now with a new engine but loaded as before to nearly 11,000 pounds, began its slow roll down Roosevelt Field in Long Island. They covered seven hundred and fifty yards and then a mile, but the plane refused to lift. Kelly slammed the T-2 to a stop, wheeled her around to another position, shoved the throttle all the way forward and hoped the heavy plane would lift above a row of hangars at the far end of the field. Tense watchers saw the T-2 groan across the roofs of the hangars and disappear from view. Aboard the plane, Kelly fought to clear the low buildings and telephone poles that dotted Long Island, as he set a westward course across New Jersey. Still flying at only 300 feet, Kelly suddenly signaled for Macready to take over inside. Macready, cursing, struggled with the interior controls to keep the plane aloft, without quite knowing where he was going. Up front, Kelly had spied trouble with the voltage regulator and patiently took the mechanism off the engine alongside him to readjust it to working condition. Macready's own efforts had been well worthwhile, for without the repairs made by his partner the T-2's batteries would never have held up for this third — and as both men knew, last—attempt to conquer the continent.

Hour after hour the big monoplane droned on, passing into the scary darkness over the Appalachians and then cutting through a heavy drizzle past St. Louis. Over Arizona, flying now in sparkling clear daylight, the flyers encountered a mountain range whose altitude obviously belied the maps they were using. Their instruments said they were at 10,000 feet, and the maps indicated the highest ground was 8,000 feet — yet dead ahead of them was a barrier they couldn't possibly surmount. For nearly an hour they looked for an opening and finally found a pass, only to discover more ridges ahead. Back they turned, this time choosing another path. Past this lay the welcome sight of flat desert, with their target city of San Diego only 300 miles ahead.

Over San Diego Kelly put the T-2's nose down and passed directly over the main street of the city. They landed to the acclaim of the populace and were handed a congratulatory telegram from President Harding. Waiting also was an offer of $5,000 made to them by an old Air Service officer who had won the cash in a bet. Kelly and Macready, both of whom had drained their own meager bank accounts to make the third trip, accepted thankfully. Their time for the 2,700-mile trip looks snail-like compared to present-day coast-to-coast flights. It was 26 hours, 50 minutes and 3 seconds.

The following year the Air Service geared for another long-range epic — this one an around-the-world attempt. Five other nations also had their eyes on a globe-girdling trip, but the United States was the only country to bring its team through to completion of the longest aerial voyage yet attempted.

No space shot of the 1960's — allowing for the technological differences of nearly a half century — ever had more work or planning put into one of its launchings than the Air Service's world-circling flight of 1924. The project was nine months in the making, during which every detail of the long course was considered. Four airplanes, called World Cruisers, were built specially for the flight by the Douglas Aircraft Company. The Cruisers carried either pontoons or wheels, a 400-horsepower Liberty engine, and enough fuel to fly 2,200 miles. The manufacturer's aim in building them was not speed (their best was 103 miles an hour) but endurance, and in this quality the Cruisers succeeded admirably. The eight aviators who volunteered for the flight — four pilots with a hand-picked mechanic for each — underwent a period of six-weeks of intensive training to sharpen up mentally and physically for the flight. Over 70 way-stations were established at which the team could stop for rest or refitting of their craft. Parts and supplies scattered along the route were meticulously crated so that the aviators could put their hands on any of the 480 items even within total blackness.

Despite all its painstaking preparations, the project nearly foundered at a number of points along the 26,000-mile route. Major Frederick Martin, overall commander of the flight and pilot of the flagplane *Seattle,* met misfortune along the cold, snowy and fog-swept coast of Alaska. Martin and his mechanic, Sergeant Alva Harvey, had started with the others well enough, but on April 16, nine days out of their departing point in Seattle, Washington, the flagplane was forced down at sea by engine trouble. Picked up by a destroyer, Martin and Harvey waited for repairs to be made and then resumed their planned series of hops along the Alaskan coast. On April 30, with its sister ships waiting for it to join them at Dutch Harbor, the *Seattle* slammed into the side of a mountain in dense fog. Luckily, neither Martin nor Harvey was seriously injured, but the men stayed in the plane wreckage for two days before they could see well enough to descend the mountain. After nearly a week of wandering they stumbled into a trapper's cabin stocked with firewood and food. There the flyers recuperated while a blizzard raged outside, and when they set out once more for civilization they were picked up by a fishing launch which observed them tramping along the shore.

Lieutenant Lowell Smith, flying the *Chicago* with Lieutenant Leslie Arnold as his mechanic, now took command of the expedition and together with the flying Cruisers *New Orleans* and *Boston* battled persistently bad weather to reach Tokyo on May 24. Winging through the warmer climes of southeast Asia, the *Chicago* came down with a cracked cylinder in a lagoon in Indochina. While natives clambered over the crippled plane, Smith and Arnold waited nervously for her sister ships to fetch help. Finally word came that a new engine was being rushed by destroyer to Hue and this time the natives turned

from hindrance to help by towing the *Chicago* upriver to the city with three sampans leading the way.

Across lower Asia the three Cruisers continued to Calcutta, where they substituted new wings and engines and switched from pontoons to landing wheels. Then they flew across the Mideast to Constantinople and on to Bucharest, Vienna and Paris. In London the six aviators braced for a difficult series of flight legs across the North Atlantic by spending two weeks in the British capital while their weary airplanes were completely overhauled. On July 30 the Cruisers landed at Kirkwall in the Orkneys and plotted their next hop to Iceland. Leaving the Scottish islands, however, they ran into thick fog. The *New Orleans,* manned by Lieutenant Erik Nelson and his companion Lieutenant John Harding, fought on to Iceland but the two other planes turned back to the Orkneys to try again the next morning. This time the weather was favorable, but soon after the second start the *Boston,* under command of pilot Lieutenant Leigh Wade and mechanic Staff Sergeant Henry Ogden, was forced down in the sea with a broken oil pump. The *Chicago* had seen the *Boston's* predicament and winged off for aid. In a few hours a Navy cruiser arrived but as it attempted to raise the stricken Douglas its boom broke; the *Boston* dropped back into the sea with a force that broke the pontoons. Watching helplessly from the ship's rail, Wade and Ogden saw the plane they had flown 19,000 miles through every conceivable kind of travail sink beneath the waves. Their spirits rose again, however, when they received news that a new Douglas Cruiser would be waiting for them in Nova Scotia so that they could complete the trip. There, furnished with the new *Boston II,* they took off with the *Chicago* and the *New Orleans* on September 5 for the final series of hops across the American continent.

Round-the-World flyers who completed the trip
(from left to right) Lts. Lowell Smith,
Henry Ogden, Erik Nelson, Leigh Wade, Jack
Harding and Leslie Arnold

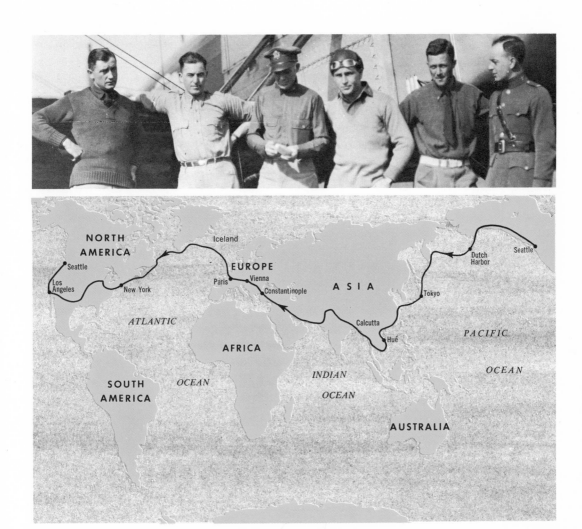

The wild reception given the pilots by Santa Monica, California, was not equalled in any of the European cities they had visited. Crowds mobbed the flyers, kissing them, pushing them and tearing hunks of cloth from their uniforms. It took a brigade of club-swinging cops to rip the men free. Then, with the shouts of a nation still ringing in their ears, the pilots headed for Seattle where they landed on September 28, 1924. For the record they had flown 26,345 miles and spent 363 hours and 6 minutes in the air.

Soon new long-range flights would make headlines. The same year an Army lieutenant, Russell Maughan, crossed America in a "dawn to dusk" series of hops. And in 1926 Navy Lieutenant Commander Richard E. Byrd electrified the world with the first flight over the North Pole. But like the Kelly-Macready flight and the Army's round the world expedition, they were forgotten as new heroes and records were proclaimed in newspaper headlines. The best reminders we have of these pilots today are the statistics of their flights . . . the cold figures. And they don't even begin to tell the story.

12
Barnstorming

The day is hot, but a crowd has already gathered at the airport to see the show. The time is the 1920's, era of bootleg whiskey, "flaming youth," and barnstorming airmen. The local airport, buzzing with activity this midsummer's day, consists of a windsock, a stubbly strip of flat field and, across the field, a corrugated metal hangar.

Out on the field four airplanes are lined up: two Curtiss Jennies, an old two-seater Army Standard trainer, and another Army castoff DH-4. The planes are aging but bright patterns of paint mask their years, the gaudy markings of a "flying circus" primed for another of its spectacular aerial exhibitions.

Lining one side of the field is a representation from the local citizenry that includes cotton-frocked women, restless youngsters darting in and out of the crowd and shirt-sleeved men, their straw hats forming shields against the sun. Some stand, some perch on black, boxy automobiles and others sit in a tiny grandstand which faces the field. Before them two airmen, chinstraps dangling from their soft leather helmets, stand talking to one another beside an idling Jenny. Abruptly they break off their conversation and climb aboard. The engine noise rises and the biplane moves rockily forward until it reaches the far end of the field. Now it wheels around with its engine blasting, picks up speed past the grandstand, and rises into the air to a chorus of kids' shouts.

Up, up the Jenny goes, all eyes following as it climbs. Far above the field, but not too far for spectators to see, a figure emerges from the front cockpit and climbs slowly through the struts and wires to the top wing. The watchers below gasp as he stands upright, remains in the same position for a moment and then walks daringly toward the wingtip. The Jenny swoops low past the grandstand, its wing-walker braced against the plane's wires. He smiles, waves, and even clowns a

bit for the crowd by raising one leg into the air as he races by at nearly 100 miles per hour. Suddenly the plane veers up sharply, the start of a loop. A cry goes up from the spectators, but the Jenny is already at the top of its maneuver and is heading toward earth again, its human cargo still glued, bolt upright, to the wing. The crowd applauds as the plane touches down for a landing.

No one leaves yet, for a man on the field shouts through a megaphone that the show is just beginning. The Standard two-seater takes off and over the field swings a figure from a narrow rope ladder attached to its landing gear; the aerial acrobat ends his stint by hanging from his teeth as the plane roars past the grandstand. Next a Jenny goes into a complicated series of acrobatics, and finally two planes maneuver close to one another while a wing-walker changes planes in midair.

At last it is the public's turn to play aviator, and a small line forms as the planes take on passengers. The fumes are overpowering, the seats uncomfortable and the risks much greater than they realize, but most folks think that the $2.50 they pay for a short haul and the $5.00 they put down for a long one is well worth it.

Such was the scene repeated, with variations, at hundreds of county fairs, carnivals, cow pastures, and summer resorts in America during the Twenties. The big money and the headlines were collected by the racers and the record-makers, the discoverers and the distance flyers. But for most airmen of the decade, making a living in aviation meant barnstorming. Barely making a living were the "gypsies" who flew alone or with a companion from town to town all over America, stunting first to attract a crowd and then taking on the paying customers as passengers. The gypsies had little use for conventional ways. They ate when they could, drank more than they should and slept under the wing of

their plane when lodgings could not be found. They had little use, moreover, for elementary safety rules, often packing passengers three abreast in a single cockpit. Members of flying troupes such as the flying circuses led a more organized existence and practiced a more elaborate set of tricks. But, in general, they too were part of the barnstorming fraternity, the carefree but skilled band of aviators who flourished during the decade after the First World War.

Most plane-watchers in the Twenties were more sophisticated than their pre-war counterparts. Dutch rolls, falling leaves, loop the loops — these were already old hat to the many hometown Americans. The air-show audiences demanded new thrills and the barnstormers often went hungry if customers weren't kept happy. One innovation was wing-walking, a particularly perilous art. Some of the wing-walkers feigned slips and near falls, to the crowd's delight. One trick was the "breakaway" in which the wing-walker suddenly "lost" his grip on wing- or landing-gear and started a sickening plunge toward earth, until a concealed cable caught his fall. One of the star wing-walkers of the Gates Flying Circus, Wesley May, once roller-skated off the top wing of a Jenny, and parachuted to earth. Seeking to perform even more astonishing tricks, he then attempted to ride a bicycle along the wing before again hitting the silk. It was the same Wesley May, flying with a barnstormer named Earl Dougherty, who in 1921 pulled off the world's first in-flight refueling demonstration. Flying in a Standard SJ-1, piloted by Frank Hawks, May, with a five-gallon can of gasoline strapped to his back, climbed from the Standard's top wing to a Jenny above. Aboard his new mount, he unstrapped the gas can and poured its contents into the Jenny's tank. The crowd at Long Beach, California, loved it.

Some of the best crowd-pleasers were the wackiest. Slats Rodgers, a lean Texas veteran of the barnstorming circuit from the time he built his own plane in 1912, devised a stunt he figured would give the audience in Wichita Falls the thrill of its life. Slats dressed a dummy to resemble an aviator — goggles, helmet and boots included — and took it aloft. Below, the crowd saw Slats' plane go into a loop and, from the forward cockpit, a figure fall out and hurtle to the earth. The object fell in the middle of the field before the spectators, who watched in horror as an ambulance raced to the scene of the disaster, picked up the "body" and wheeled off to the nearest hospital with a police escort showing the way. When Slats landed, he was hauled off for an interview with the sheriff who, it turned out, had liked the show so much he couldn't think of any charges to press.

Another zany stunt, touched with the same dash of the morbid, was dreamed up by a barnstormer named William (Wild Bill) Kopia. Kopia donned the fancy clothes of a female "opera star" and purchased a ticket for a ride. Once safely ensconced in the plane's cockpit, the pilot pretended to have forgotten something, and climbed down. Meantime, its engine idling, the plane burst forward to the accompanying screeches of the "singer." Up it went into the sky, running through a series of outlandish stunts, but manning the dual controls all the time was Bill Kopia.

Accidents were bound to happen to the barnstormers, and they often did. Nearly all the planes in use were of wartime vintage and they were weary from hard flying and haphazard maintenance. Planes were given replacement parts from whatever make was available, and the only fuel used was the only one available, automobile gasoline. They rarely had shelter; accident reports listing rotten fabric or structural failure were common during the heyday of the gypsy flyers.

Barnstormers and gypsy flyers
followed the circuit of state fairs
performing dazzling feats of acrobatic flying and
dangerous mid-air transfers

On the other hand, the wood and fabric construction of surplus aircraft saved many a barnstormer's life in a crash. When they cracked up they crumpled in a mass of wires, broken wood and shredded cloth which absorbed much of the shock of impact. More than one barnstormer walked away from such a junkheap that bore no resemblance to the original airplane.

One who lived to fly again after several barnstorming crashes was Charles A. Lindbergh, nicknamed "The Flying Fool" during his brief barnstorming career. Lindbergh was a rawboned youngster when he and a companion decided to make a transcontinental tour in 1923 in a Canadian Jenny. This plane, known as a "Canuck," featured slightly more zip than the Jenny plus a pair of clipped wings. The pilots' first mishap occurred when they collided with a sand hillock near Pensacola, Florida, rendering the plane battered but repairable. In Texas Lindbergh and his companion had trouble getting off the ground because in order to increase range they had strapped bulky fuel tanks aboard the fuselage, adding both weight and drag to the plane. The plane ran out of fuel over the town of Camp Wood, Texas, and the Canuck had to be set down in the town square. The landing was made without a hitch, but the takeoff presented a problem. The square wasn't wide enough for a good takeoff run, so Lindbergh started well back on a side street in order to build up speed. He and the Canuck negotiated the narrow street all right, but when he tried to squeeze between two telephone poles his wing tip caught one, spinning the ship through the window of a local hardware store. Lindbergh climbed out, expecting a fat bill from the merchant. Instead, the hardware man seemed delighted. The publicity would be great for business, he told the astonished young flyer. Farther west they set the Canuck down on the desert for the night, but on taking off the next morning they met another obstacle, this time in the form of a tall cactus. Soon after this the trouble-plagued pair abandoned their crosscountry journey. Lindbergh was to have better luck heading in the opposite direction four years later.

Lindbergh was one of several airmen nurtured in barnstorming but destined for bigger and better things. Another was Wiley Post, the round-the-world aviator of the early 1930's who was dubbed "The Flying Redskin" in his wing-walking days. Frank Hawks, who participated in the first in-flight refueling demonstration, became known as a speed flyer a decade later. Ben O. Howard was a noted racing pilot and designer after an early career as an aerial bootlegger. Mort Bach was one of several daredevil flyers who became airline or airplane-manufacturing executives. And then there was Frank Clarke, a virtuoso stunter, who went on to a colorful career as a Hollywood stunt flyer.

"Spooks" Clarke got his start in 1918 at Venice Field near Los Angeles where he performed everything from wing-walking to plane-changing to the bizarre act of leaping from the tail of a plane into its cockpit. Soon the dapper, mustachioed Clarke was trying more difficult stunts like grabbing a rope trailing from a plane overhead as he ran along the ground, or climbing back to the tail of a plane and manipulating its controls by rope.

His very first Hollywood assignment in 1920 had Clarke's stamp of derring-do on it. Dressed as a policeman, he chased stunter Mark Campbell in convict's stripes from cockpit to wing, through the undercarriage and back up the other side. The plane flew on during the chase with its controls lashed in neutral. In a stunt concocted for a film called *Stranger than Fiction* he easily topped his premiere performance. Perching a Jenny atop the thirteen-story Railroad Building in downtown Los Angeles, Clarke revved the plane across a narrow wooden runway as camera crews cranked away to record the feat. At the end of the track the Jenny jumped off a slight incline and then dipped perilously toward the street below. But Clarke had the plane quickly under control and merrily waggled his wings at the open-mouthed crowd as he soared away.

Some of Clarke's aerial maneuvers verged on insanity. There is the story about his passion for a nightclub singer in Tucson, Arizona, and how he flew his plane up to her apartment window, rolled its wheels alongside the building and tossed in a love letter. And there was the time he decided to climb out of the cockpit, along the fuselage and out on the wings, hands tied together. Clarke slipped sometimes, but this time it was not planned. As he was swept back he was snagged in a wire, which saved him from certain death.

Clarke's consummate flying skill saved the life of a fellow-flyer on more than one occasion, but none of his rescues was more spectacular than the time he caught a falling body with his plane, like an outfielder gathering in a fly ball. Stunter Al Wilson was to make a plane change from a ship manned by Wally Timm above to Clarke's which was coming up from below and behind. As Clarke made his approach, though, Wilson lost his grip and started falling — minus parachute — toward the earth 5,000 feet below. Clarke put his plane into a violent dive, maneuvered under the plummeting Wilson and snared him head first in one wing. That's the way Wilson stayed until they reached the ground.

In 1927 Clarke led a crew of some 40 stunt pilots in several months of aerial dog-fighting filming *Hell's Angels*. The Howard Hughes epic spared no expense to record some of the greatest aerial dogfights ever filmed, with an assortment of decade-old SE-5's, Fokker D-VII's, Curtiss Canucks, Sopwith Camels and other war-surplus crates taking part. Three flyers died in the filming, not from mock machine guns mounted aboard the planes but from the frantic maneuvers they were called upon to make in the name of realism. Clarke, who played Baron von Richthofen, completed the filming unscathed but sobered by the experience.

The famed Hollywood stunter continued active until his own sense of humor caught up with him one day in 1948. Buzzing an old friend, he rolled his ship over at low altitude with the intention of dropping a sack of manure on his buddy's land. Clarke's war-surplus Vultee Valiant went into its roll but suddenly plunged into the ground with a terrific explosion. When the bodies of Clarke and that of a companion were removed, the manure sack was found wedged behind the control stick — a joke turned tragically sour.

The Hollywood aerial fraternity to which Clarke belonged also included such renowned stunters as Dick Grace, Art Goebel, Hank Coffin and Paul Mantz, to name but a few. The millions who watched them perform in early newsreels or in such later films as *Wings, Lilac Time,* and *Dawn Patrol* never knew the genuine dangers the stunters faced when flying before the cameras. For the movie-goer, relaxing in his theater seat, they made it look easy.

13
Airplane in Ascendancy

The United States found itself trailing the nations of Europe in an important new aviation development after World War I. The land of the Wright brothers' seminal flight relinquished the head start it had gained in 1903 to European air progress during the latter part of the decade, then fell markedly behind Europe during the war. As the world settled back to peace America could boast of a few brilliant record-making flights which ranged across the Atlantic, over the American continent and around the world. But they were seen as individual triumphs, pointing the way to the distant future perhaps, but having little connection with the lives of average citizens.

After the Armistice, several European nations moved quickly into a major new field: commercial aviation. Airlines began operating in four countries within a year after the guns fell silent. In freshly defeated Germany an air service sprang up in February 1919 linking Berlin, Leipzig and Weimar. France's Henri Farman inaugurated a passenger service from Paris to London a few days later, serving a champagne luncheon to passengers as they gazed down at the English Channel. Three British airlines followed suit with daily schedules between the capitals, and late in the year the Dutch launched their Royal Dutch Airlines (KLM) under government auspices.

America's failure to follow the same course could be laid to several factors. For one, the immense distances between key cities simply couldn't be negotiated with equipment available. For another, running a passenger or freight airline meant making a profit, and the number of passengers, or the quantity of cargo which could be put aboard one of the flying crates of the post-war era (there *were* a few persons willing to risk their necks) did not begin to pay the costs of running such a service. Still another factor relating directly to costs of operation was the reluctance of the United States government to involve itself in

an air-subsidy program. The French and the Dutch, notable among the European nations, had recognized that some form of financial nourishment would be needed to sustain their infant airlines. Americans resisted the idea; theirs was a land of free enterprise where government subsidy was likely to be looked upon more as meddling than assistance. A few commercial operations did crop up after war's end but they were aerial ferries from cities to resorts, short distanced and short lived. Small flying boats took vacationers from New York to Atlantic City, for instance, and from Los Angeles to Catalina Island. They soon ceased to operate from lack of profit. Only when business had joined hands with government in a subsidy program of sorts — involving a healthy return of airmail revenues to private carriers — did commercial aviation begin to grow. By then more than half the decade had passed.

The real seeds of commercial aviation were sown in another part of the aviation domain — the U.S. Aerial Mail Service. It was the brave pilots of the Air Mail, flying outmoded machines under the worst conditions, who blazed a trail across the nation for the airlines to follow. Air Mail planes carried the first few passengers across the country's vital routes. The Air Mail made it economically possible for private business to enter the aviation picture, ushering in a new era.

The official opening of Air Mail service was anything but encouraging. The date was May 15, 1918, hardly a favorable moment in the history of the nation for starting the project. The war was on, and considerable criticism had been voiced over launching an experiment in airmail. But time was running out on the summer deadline Congress had set when it appropriated $100,000 to see if the airmail idea would work. And so, on that fine spring morning Army aviators readied their Curtiss Jennies at three separate points along the

Final briefing before first airmail flight from
Washington's Potomac Park, May 15, 1918.
President Wilson attended ceremonies

"Boyle was overhead and turning as he climbed," Lipsner recalled later. "I watched him for some minutes, trying to figure out what he was doing. Finally I realized that he was taking a course that was almost opposite to the one he had been instructed to fly. The first scheduled air mail was in the air — but it was flying in the wrong direction."

Apparently the only one who noticed Boyle's error, Lipsner sat down in his office and waited in misery for the next news. It wasn't long in coming.

"Captain Lipsner?" said a voice over the phone. It was Boyle. "My compass got a little mixed up. I just landed a while ago here at Waldorf, Maryland."

"What about the mail?" Lipsner asked.

"It's being loaded into a car now," Boyle said. "It's going to be driven back to Washington."

East Coast. The plan was to fly the mail in opposite directions from Washington and New York, with a midpoint relay in Philadelphia for each flight. In New York Lieutenant Torrey Webb took off in fine style. In Washington Lieutenant George L. Boyle climbed aboard his plane, adjusted his helmet, and shouted "Contact!" Mechanics swung the wooden prop — and nothing happened. Again they tried, and again, until their arms grew weary. Not far from the plane President Woodrow Wilson fidgeted, obviously annoyed at the delay. The captain in charge conferred nervously with the chief mechanic. Someone checked the gas tank; it was empty. Men scurried to correct the oversight, and when the plane was fueled, it burst into life and taxied across the field for takeoff. Boyle took her up low over a line of trees at the end of the field, giving everyone in attendance a moment of fright. But at last the Jenny was airborne and gaining altitude. The President and his wife headed toward their car and the crowd began to disperse. Capt. Benjamin Lipsner breathed a sigh of relief now that the first worrisome moments of his project were over, and was heading for the hangar when he turned back for a last look at the mail plane.

To everyone's surprise, the Army soon built a record of steady service between New York and Washington. Its role, however, was designed to give the Air Mail a start; after three months it turned over operations to the Post Office Department. Lipsner resigned from the service to become the first Air Mail Superintendent, and immediately began putting the service on a civilian footing. Among his first steps was the hiring of civilian pilots and the purchase of six new Standard biplanes to supplement the surplus warplanes then available. Together with Jennies and DH-4's, the Standards comprised the backbone of the early Air Mail fleet.

The Air Mail made its first long haul in September 1918 when pilots Max Miller and Ed Gardner manned separate planes across the feared "hell stretch" of the Allegheny Mountains. Miller and Gardner carried 400 pounds of mail apiece on the New York to Chicago flight, arriving safely at their destination after suffering engine breakdowns, missed landmarks and numerous forced landings.

Impatient with old-line thinking, Gen. "Billy" Mitchell brought about his own court-martial by denouncing the country's military and civil aviation policies

A more ambitious span was planned in 1921, when two flights each, out of New York and San Francisco, were to travel cross-country in a series of continuous relays to the opposite coasts. The westbound flights ran into heavy snow and only one reached Chicago where it was forced to stop. The eastbound team out of San Francisco lost a pilot when he dived to his death in Nevada. But the other flight kept going until it relayed its way to New York in 33 hours and 20 minutes. It was this flight which provided the occasion for one of aviation's greatest moments, when Jack Knight flew through night and snow across unfamiliar ground, from North Platte, Nebraska, to Chicago. In so doing "Skinny" Knight, who had refused to halt his flight even though a relief pilot did not show up along the route, gave the Air Mail Service a much needed publicity boost in its effort to extract a new appropriation from Congress.

The transcontinental mail relay showed that regular coast-to-coast service would some day be practical, but it also illustrated some fundamental weaknesses in the state of aviation at the time. Landing fields were too scarce, and aids to night flying almost non-existent. As a result, the Post Office Department laid out a network of emergency landing fields along the routes. It also asked the Sperry Gyroscope Company to develop powerful revolving beacons that were to become "lighthouses of the sky" across the country.

Even more pressing was the aircraft problem. The war types in use were no substitute for the kind of planes needed to perform across long distances, through the black of night and in foul weather. DH-4's were improved by shifting the pilot away from the biplane's notorious gas tank to the rear cockpit (the DH-4 never shook its "Flaming Coffin" nickname), adding night lights and strengthening the landing gear. But modifica-

tions like these were only stopgap measures. New designs were needed, yet the Air Mail Service, operating at a loss with scarcely enough funds to keep running, was in no position to support a technological development program. Time and the course of events were to change that. Before the decade was over, American aviation received an infusion of ideas and money which created new ferment in the industry and led directly to the birth of the airlines.

Helping pave the way to commercial aviation in the United States was — unexpectedly — the court martial of one of America's most famous airmen, Billy Mitchell. The outspoken Mitchell, long a thorn in the side of tradition-minded officers because of his advocacy of air power, had stunned the defenders of naval superiority in 1921 with his bombing demonstrations off the Virginia capes. Using the former German battleship *Ostfriesland* as a target, Mitchell's Martin bombers polished off the big ship in two brief installments. Four years later, in 1925, Mitchell dropped a verbal blockbuster on the military establishment with a slashing attack on the Navy's handling of an attempt by three flying boats to reach Hawaii from California. None made it; in the worst mishap one lost its bearings, ditched in the sea and drifted helplessly for 10 days before being picked up. "These accidents are the direct results of incompetency, criminal negligence and almost treasonable administration of the National Defense by the Navy and War Departments," said Mitchell in a long and bitterly worded statement. Few were surprised when a court martial resulted. The trial lasted two months and ended in Mitchell's suspension from the military service. Conducted in the glare of press coverage, the trial fixed national attention on the officer's charges. Was there "criminal negligence" of military aviation? Was it so, as Mitchell had said, that "our pilots know they are going

to be killed if they stay in the service, on account of the methods employed, in the old floating coffins that we are still flying?"

Even before the trial was over an Aircraft Inquiry Board was looking at military and civil aviation practices. The Morrow Board (called after its chairman, Dwight Morrow) did not agree with Mitchell's longtime advocacy of a separate air force; this had to wait until after World War II to become a reality. But it did make recommendations to improve military and civil aviation, among them a recommendation that the Department of Commerce take a hand in the development of commercial aviation. As a result Congress passed an act the following year establishing a Bureau of Aeronautics in the Department and setting up regulations that played an important part in commercial aviation's future.

The real turning point toward creating the airlines came from a slightly earlier piece of legislation, the Air Mail Act of 1925. Called the Kelly Act after its sponsor, Representative Clyde Kelly of Pennsylvania, this measure gave the Postmaster General the authority to contract for airmail service with private air operators. The practice of parceling out airmail work to private lines was not exactly new. William Boeing, a wealthy young sportsman with an interest in flying, had run the first private airmail project in 1919 with his partner Eddie Hubbard, carrying mail between ocean liners and Seattle. At least two other private carriers also worked out-of-the-way routes. But the Kelly Act took the whole airmail operation out of the hands of the Post Office Department and turned it over to private business. The Department first set up short "feeder" routes between various cities and scheduled the start of a transcontinental "Columbia" route once the short lines were working satisfactorily. Businessmen, lured by the Kelly Act's allowance of 80 percent of airmail revenue to the con-

Airmail feeder routes were contracted to
private operators in 1926. The transcontinental express
sections were set up in 1927 and commercial air travel
across the United States became a reality

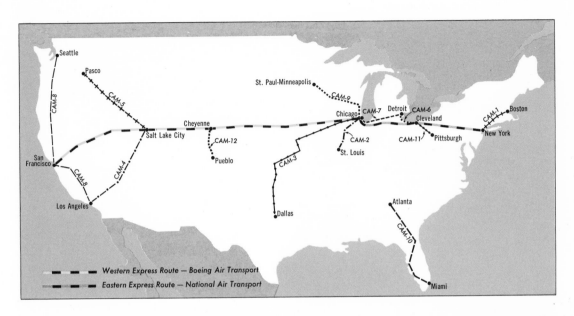

Western Express Route — Boeing Air Transport
Eastern Express Route — National Air Transport

tractor who carried it, flooded the Post Office Department with more than 5,000 bids. From these the Department chose the operators of 12 feeder or CAM (Contract Air Mail) routes linking cities throughout the nation.

The opening of the Columbia route in 1927 provided further stimulus to commercial aviation. Boeing won the western segment from the West Coast to Chicago, and eventually joined hands with the engine-makers Pratt and Whitney to form United Aircraft; United soon won controlling interest in the carrier along the eastern segment of the transcontinental route, National Air Transport. Boeing's advent into commercial aviation had other far-reaching effects. To hurdle the high Rockies he produced a new airplane, the Boeing 40, powered by the new "Wasp" radial engine and equipped to carry two passengers in addition to its mail cargo. The B-40 pointed the way to even bigger and faster planes — the Fokker and Ford trimotors of the late Twenties.

The Air Mail contracts provided the genesis for several of the modern airlines. Colonial Air Lines, which won CAM Route No. 1

between New York and Boston, was the predecessor of American Airlines. Western Express, operator of CAM-4 from Los Angeles to Salt Lake, eventually became part of TWA. Northwest Airlines picked up CAM-9 from Chicago to Minneapolis after its original contractor gave it up. In addition to National Air Transport, United absorbed the operators of two western routes, Varney Lines which had won CAM-5, and Pacific Air Transport, operator of CAM-8. And in the midwest, the biggest name in automobiles, Henry Ford, emerged as a major force on the aviation scene by winning the contracts for CAM-6 and CAM-7 between Detroit, Chicago and Cleveland. Ford's advent into aviation gave a skeptical public new confidence in air transport — if the astute auto manufacturer was willing to get into the business there must be something to it.

Even greater public faith was inspired by an event in 1927. That year an obscure airmail pilot, who had been making the CAM-2 run between St. Louis and Chicago, flew alone across the Atlantic Ocean. His flight was to open a new phase in aviation history.

14
Flight of Flights

Nature seemed to conspire against Charles A. Lindbergh as he warmed up his Ryan monoplane that gray morning of May 20, 1927. Rain had soaked Roosevelt Field in Long Island during the night, turning the sandy clay of its runway into a soft and springless surface. Minutes before, a slight headwind favorable for takeoff had changed to a tailwind. And to make matters worse, the *Spirit of St. Louis'* radial engine was registering 30 revolutions too low on the instrument panel before Lindbergh's eyes. His mechanic reminded him that the Wright Whirlwind was merely protesting the wet weather, but that was little satisfaction for a pilot about to take off with an overload of fuel on a trip across the vast Atlantic Ocean.

Bad breaks were nothing new for the lanky young flyer from the midwest. As a barnstormer and later as an Army airman serving a brief hitch in Texas, Lindbergh had learned to withstand — and survive — the perils of

flying. Ever since he had been bitten by the transatlantic bug while transporting the mail between St. Louis and Chicago the year before, one obstacle after another seemed to stand in his way. Determined to make the flight, he had surmounted each one. It wasn't Raymond Orteig's prize offer of $25,000 that made the long hop so attractive. Lindbergh had a love of flying, a desire to excel in his art, and a profound faith in the future of aviation. He was sure a nonstop ocean crossing from New York to Paris would advance aviation as no other flight ever had.

From the start Lindbergh decided he would make the crossing in a single-engine plane. Wouldn't a multi-engine craft, say a Fokker trimotor, be more certain to get across? His St. Louis backers had asked the young pilot some rather penetrating questions on that account. No, said Lindbergh, multi-engine planes were more complicated and expensive. They handled harder in rough

As the *Spirit of St. Louis* lifted slowly above Roosevelt Field a drama began which did not end until "Lone Eagle," Charles A. Lindbergh, touched down in Paris 33 hours later

weather and besides, the loss of an engine over the middle of the ocean would probably prevent him from reaching land anyway. Still, Lindbergh had asked the Fokker company for a price on their airplane and had been given one he couldn't possible meet — $90,000. He had tried hard to buy a Bellanca monoplane, but the deal had fallen through after the owner demanded the right to pick the crew. The eager flyer had also received a quick turndown from a midwest manufacturer, Travel Air. And so he had turned to a small west coast concern that made mail planes, Ryan Airlines. Ryan said it could build the plane Lindbergh wanted in two months for $6,000 plus engine. The young airman figured total costs at something over $10,000. With a $15,000 check from his St. Louis backers in his pocket, Lindbergh told the Ryan company to go ahead.

While Lindbergh pored over details of design with Ryan's chief engineer, Donald Hall, a number of other flyers set their sights on an Atlantic venture. Each was nearer readiness than Lindbergh. One expedition was led by Lieutenant Commander Noel Davis, who was to fly a Keystone trimotor, the *American Legion*. Richard Byrd, aerial conquerer of the North Pole, was readying a Fokker trimotor named *America* for the trip, while a third flight boasting the Bellanca Lindbergh had sought, now named *Columbia,* was being prepared by onetime barnstormer Clarence Chamberlin. A fourth flight involved the French war ace Charles Nungesser who planned to fly in the opposite direction, from Paris to New York.

Lindbergh kept following reports of their progress, figuring that if any of them made the crossing he would change his plans and fly across the Pacific. In April 1927 the *American Legion* cracked up on its final test flight, killing Davis and his navigator. Byrd's Fokker also crashed on a test flight, causing no

fatalities but sustaining enough damage to set back departure plans. The Nungesser flight disappeared over the Atlantic and was never seen again. In the Chamberlin camp bickering broke out over the choice of crew.

At the Ryan plant Lindbergh and Hall worked steadily on. There would be no feuding on this project. Not only had the businessmen putting up their money given Lindbergh a free hand in all details, but the sober-faced young flyer from Minnesota would have no crew problems. He wanted to make the trip alone, he told Hall, when the designer asked him where he wanted cockpits for himself and the navigator. "I only want one cockpit," Lindbergh had replied. "I'll do the navigating myself." In place of the extra man he preferred more fuel. He needed that as insurance for the long crossing.

The *Spirit of St. Louis* was a custom-made airplane from start to finish. Lindbergh wanted no frills in the cockpit, just a wicker seat, his instruments, windows on either side and a skylight overhead. Because he didn't want to be sandwiched between engine and gas tanks in a crackup, a fuel tank rode ahead of the pilot, just where the windshield should be. This gave the plane a blind spot directly ahead, but Lindbergh said he could get what forward view he needed from the side windows. The plane could carry 450 gallons of gas and do 120 miles per hour with its 237-horsepower Whirlwind wide open. It was graceful in appearance, but unstable in flight — a factor that helped keep its pilot awake when he was trying to ward off sleep on the long trip to Europe. The *Spirit of St. Louis* was not a novice's airplane, but that didn't matter. No one but Lindbergh ever flew it.

Lindbergh had plenty of practice with his plane by the time he was ready to depart; he'd flown it cross-country in two headline-making segments from the west coast to St.

Richard E. Byrd   Charles Nungesser

Louis and from that city to New York. But it was strange to his touch that momentous spring morning of May 20th. "The *Spirit of St. Louis* feels more like an overloaded truck than an airplane," he thought to himself as he headed down the runway on Roosevelt Field. An eternity seemed to pass before the airplane's wheels lifted off the soggy ground . . . until it cleared a row of telephone wires at the end of the field. Once aloft, Lindbergh found surprisingly good response in controls in spite of the fact that the Ryan's wing was supporting 5,000 pounds of airplane, fuel and pilot. He pointed its nose northeast along the great circle route to Paris and passed over the American coastline under clearing skies.

By noon Lindbergh was over Nova Scotia, wondering if anyone had spotted his plane, and a few hours later he winged over the rugged coastline of Newfoundland. Beyond was open sea — that lonely expanse from which there could be no turning back. He noted for the first time that he already had a powerful desire to sleep. There had been precious little chance for that the night before. Friends had taken him to see the Broadway show *Rio Rita* but before the party arrived at the theater someone had remembered to check the weather. After weeks of storms, the weather bureau now reported, the forecast was for clearing across the Atlantic with local storms only. Acutely aware that both Byrd and Chamberlin also were waiting for the weather to break, Lindbergh hurried back to Roosevelt Field. He had lain down for a couple of hours but sleep wouldn't come. Now, over the trackless seas, when the steady drone of his engine was the only sound he heard, Lindbergh yearned for rest. For a time the combination of flying and threatening weather kept mind and body alert. He climbed over a thick fog, then ran into cold masses of clouds. Ice formed on the wing and for awhile he feared his instruments had

stopped functioning. Past the clouds, though, waves of sleep returned. Groggy, he flew on through the night, telling himself over and over that if he didn't stay awake, "there's no alternative but death and failure." Once the plane began falling out of control and the pilot brought it level with a jolt. A little later the desire to sleep became so overpowering that Lindbergh stuck his head out a side window and let the slipstream's blast of air wash over his face. That seemed to turn the trick; awareness began to return.

Still over the ocean 26 hours out of New York Lindbergh spotted a small fleet of fishing boats and circled down to shout, "Which way to Ireland?" One head appeared from a cabin and seemed to stare dumbly back. Nonplussed, Lindbergh resumed his course. He passed over Ireland with a sense of elation and a growing feeling of confidence. If Paris were socked in, he mused, he might even fly on to Rome. What a surprise that would be to the people back home!

It was just past 10 p.m. in Paris when the sound of the *Spirit of St. Louis* was heard above the city. Lindbergh hunted for signs of Le Bourget Aerodrome, which he had been told he couldn't miss if he flew northeast from the city. He puzzled at the rows of lights radiating from the field, then concentrated his dulled senses on the job of landing at night on an unfamiliar runway. The *Spirit of St. Louis* had touched down and had begun taxiing toward a hangar when it was surrounded by a wave of humanity. A massive crowd had gathered at the airport to welcome him. The traffic jam that ensued explained the lights seen by Lindbergh. The pilot cut the switch and looked out on a sea of faces shouting in accents strange to his ears. Behind him he heard the sounds of ripping fabric and cracking wood — the souvenir hunters had already gone to work. He opened the door and stepped out, but was caught up

immediately by the crowd and carried off. His flight was over almost 33½ hours after he had left New York.

The honors, more fittingly the worship, accorded Lindbergh must be recorded as unique in the history of man. Although officially ineligible for the Orteig prize (the required 60 days between entry and flight had not elapsed), he was awarded the check without hesitation by the prize committee. Home again with his plane, which was shipped back aboard the cruiser *Memphis,* the young hero embarked on a flying tour of the nation which covered 22,350 miles and stops in 82 cities. He spoke about aviation and its future importance; and wherever he went crowds hailed and officials honored him. Cities groomed airports to greet him and those without facilities built them. The flight of the "Lone Eagle" stirred the nation to greater enthusiasm for aviation than ever before.

A burst of activity followed the Lindbergh flight. In June, two weeks after the *Spirit of St. Louis'* crossing, Clarence Chamberlin flew from New York to Germany aboard the same Bellanca Lindbergh had turned down during his search for a plane to make the trip. A few days later Richard Byrd and his crew of three attempted a New York to Paris flight in their Fokker trimotor, but had to settle for a forced landing in heavy fog off the French coast.

That June of 1927 also saw another Fokker blaze a trail from the California coast to Hawaii. The demanding journey, requiring pinpoint navigation, was made by two Army flyers, Lieutenants Lester G. Maitland and Albert F. Hegenberger.

Lindbergh's own journey touched off a new boom in commercial aviation as well. The year after his crossing, mail loads trebled and the number of passengers flying American lines quadrupled. Investors hurried to put their money into the budding airlines. Suddenly, aviation was becoming big business.

15
Unlimited Horizons

The value of long distance flights diminished after Charles Lindbergh made his epic crossing of the Atlantic. Ocean crossings became frequent, and far-flung trips across isolated parts of the world became commonplace. It took a flight like Wiley Post's round-the-world trip in 1933, made in his Lockheed Vega "Winnie Mae," to capture the public imagination. Four years later a freckle-faced aviatrix named Amelia Earhart gave the world a moment of heartbreak when she and her navigator were lost in the Pacific during a globe-circling attempt.

But increasingly, it was the engineer with a slide rule, rather than the pilot in the skies, who assumed importance as the decade of the Thirties dawned. Airplane speeds were becoming greater, ranges more distant and altitudes higher. The public still thrilled to the daring achievements of individual airmen and airwomen, but aircraft progress now depended upon scientific advances in such areas as engine technology, aerodynamics and metallurgy. The rapid progress made in those fields since the Twenties has wrought a revolution in aircraft which has pushed our goals from the air above to the trackless space beyond the earth's atmosphere.

Even as Lindbergh flew the Atlantic, the foundations of two momentous developments were being laid in remote corners of the aviation world. One of them was the gas-turbine jet engine, a concept which eliminated the propeller and relied on the thrust of exhaust gases for propulsion. Another was the rocket engine, which is the conversion of an age-old explosive device into a powerful aerial motor.

The modern jet engine stems from the turbine theories of a British engineer, Dr. A. A. Griffith, in 1926 and from the jet engine patent of a young Royal Air Force officer, Frank Whittle, in 1930. For several years after receiving his patent, Whittle tried to raise money to develop the idea, without much success. Adding to his frustration was the British government's official indifference. "Scientific investigation into the possibilities has given no indication that this method can be a serious competitor to the airscrew-engine combination," said the British Under Secretary of State for Air in 1934. By 1937, however, Whittle had put together enough financial backing to run a test on his newly constructed jet. During several trials, the flaming monster ran out of control while its inventor stood by paralyzed with fright. The engine held enough promise for the government to become interested, and in 1939 a new test series was launched with official support. A year and a half after Britain went to war with Germany a Whittle engine first powered an airplane in flight. The date was May 15, 1941.

A few forward-looking Germans also were interested in jet propulsion. In 1936 the Heinkel aircraft company hired a young physicist named Hans von Ohain to develop his own newly patented jet. Like Whittle, von Ohain was disappointed with his initial tests. But by 1939 the company had produced a satisfactory turbojet engine and installed it in a Heinkel He-178 fighter. The plane was demonstrated before a skeptical contingent of German officers in August of 1939 but failed to make much of an impression. The beginning of World War II five days later gave Nazi leaders second thoughts, however. By 1942, Germany had produced a new jet engine and installed it in the prototype of its first operational jet fighter, the Me-262A.

The application of rocket power to controlled flight also goes back to the Twenties. The use of rockets for aerial displays dates back at least to the 13th century; a form of rocket was used in warfare by the Arabs as early as the 7th century. Early in this century, theories on the use of rockets for space flight were advanced by the German,

The first flight of Whittle jet engine installed in a Gloster aircraft took place at Cranwell, England, on May 15, 1941

Hermann Oberth, and the Russian, K. E. Tsiolkovsky, who wrote in 1903 that rockets fueled by liquid propellants must be the means for space travel.

It was an American, Dr. Robert H. Goddard, who put theory into practice by firing the world's first liquid-propellant rocket in 1926. The flight, which was made in Auburn, Massachusetts, traveled 184 feet in two and a half seconds. In 1929 the modest professor of physics started a new series of tests in which one flight climbed to 2,000 feet at a rate of 500 miles an hour. Dr. Goddard's most important contributions were made in the field of flight control rather than in speed or distance. He is credited with the first use of gyroscopically controlled guide vanes in the exhaust stream, later used by the Germans in their V-2 guided missile of World War II.

Like the development of jet engines and modern rocketry, the major steps toward the improvement of conventional aircraft took place in the relative obscurity of scientific laboratories and engineering workshops. The monoplane replaced the biplane after 1930 by virtue of the unbraced-cantilever wing (first used in the German Junkers fighter of 1915) and an understanding of the effects of drag. Progress in metallurgy resulted in the replacement of wood and fabric by all-metal, stressed-skin construction. Improved liquid-cooled engines were tailored to the lines of streamlined fuselages; radial engines were covered by low-drag cowlings. Retractable landing gear were widely introduced in the mid-Thirties. Improvements in propellers were underlined by the introduction of variable-pitch and constant-speed mechanisms.

Unlike jet and rocket research, however, conventional piston-engine aircraft were constantly in the public view. Often the very uses to which airplanes were put helped hasten new developments. Military aircraft had to be built to meet the demands of warfare and

to keep pace with rival nations. Increasing numbers of private citizens bought their own light airplanes, emphasizing the need for safe design and construction. And the gaudy air races of the Twenties and Thirties served both as a proving ground for innovations and an incentive for better airplanes.

The big racing contests of the era were the Schneider Trophy Race and the National Air Races, and they were unmatched by any sport for excitement. At worst, they were Roman carnivals of thrills and spills. Three pilots and a spectator were killed and a dozen onlookers injured in the 1930 National Air Races in Chicago. At best, though, they fielded some superb airplanes which foretold things to come. Two of the sleekest designs of the period, the American Curtiss biplane racer and the British Supermarines S-5 and S-6 monoplanes, were winners of Schneider races. The Curtiss, whose 1925 victory was achieved with Army Lieutenant James Doolittle at the controls, gave birth to the famous line of Hawk fighters. The Supermarines were father to the legendary British Spitfire fighter whose speed and all-around capabilities checked the German Luftwaffe's London blitz during World War II. After taking permanent possession of the Schneider cup, the pontoon-equipped Supermarine S-6B cracked the world's speed record in 1931 by racing a then fantastic 407.5 m.p.h.

The National Air Races inspired a number of flying freaks, such as the Granville Brothers' Gee Bee, a barrel-shaped "flying silo" which won the 1932 Thompson speed trophy under Doolittle's skilled command. Built around a powerful radial Wasp engine, the Gee Bee design proved to be too hot to handle; every one ever built crashed. Better designs gained equal fame, such as Roscoe Turner's Wedell-Williams racer, winner of the 1933 Bendix cross-country trophy and the 1934 Thompson trophy, and the all-metal

Commercial airliners 1933-1969
(top to bottom) Boeing 247, Douglas DC-3,
Boeing 314 Clipper, Boeing 707 Jetliner,
Boeing 747 Superjet

Seversky P-35 pursuit plane, victor in the Bendix in 1937, '38 and 39.

Although it never actually entered a National Air Race, the H-1 single engine speedster of millionaire Howard Hughes set a high standard for contestants to match. The H-1, as cleanly designed as it was beautiful, made a dash of over 352 m.p.h. in 1935 to break the 3 km speed record, but its pilot-owner mercifully withdrew it from the Thompson the following year when some entrants protested its clear superiority. The H-1, which also set a cross-country record in 1937, was loaded with innovations which included a flush riveted metal fuselage and jet thrust exhaust.

Commercial aircraft reflected the advancing technology of the times in two notable designs. One was the Boeing 247, a 10-passenger low wing monoplane capable of cruising at about 185 m.p.h. The other was the Douglas DC-2, a 14-passenger plane of similar configuration which cruised at about 190 m.p.h. These all-metal transports, both equipped with retractable landing gear, represented a marked improvement over earlier airliners and started a new phase in air travel. The DC-3, which succeeded the DC-2 in 1935, became the workhorse of airlines all over the world. It went on to chalk up a distinguished military record during World War II, and continued in the service of many small airlines as late as the 1960's.

Flying boats wrote a significant chapter in aircraft development before the war. Models built by the Sikorsky, Martin and Boeing companies in the United States, by the Short Brothers in Britain, and by the Dornier and Blohm und Voss concerns in Germany paved commercial aviation's way across the oceans. Boeing's giant B-314 Yankee Clipper, introduced in 1938, provided an escape route for hundreds of European refugees as World War II broke out. But for all its promise, the flying boat became a casualty of the war.

When peace resumed, its intercontinental role was taken over by new long-range landplanes.

World War II gave a great boost to aircraft development, not only in the refinement of conventional types but in the first practical use of helicopters and the emergence of jet airplanes. Fighters entered the war with top speeds of around 350 m.p.h. At the close of hostilities in 1945 planes like the late version of the Spitfire, Germany's Me-109 and Focke-Wulf FW-190, and the United States' North American Mustang P-51 were doing approximately 450 m.p.h. Bomber design improved too. By war's end, America's Boeing B-29, with a range of 4,100 miles and speed of 350 m.p.h., was dumping bomb loads of 20,000 pounds on German and Japanese cities. New uses were found for existing aircraft which had far-reaching effects. The old biplane found a role as trainer, and the DC-3 and its successor, the DC-4, as troop and cargo transports. The glider made a comeback as a troop carrier under the tow of bombers or transports. The helicopter began its career of diverse duties.

Most important to the future of aviation, however, was the advent of the jet. During the war, propeller-driven planes reached the limit of their capabilities; beyond speeds of 450 m.p.h., engineers knew, their efficiency was sharply reduced. Before the war was over their successors—the jets—were in the skies. Britain's entry was the twin-jet Gloster Meteor, and Germany's, the twin-engine Me-262 as well as the V-1 flying bomb, driven by the pulse-jet engine, a variation of the turbo-jet. Intense work on military jet designs continued after the war, but because of high costs of converting from piston-engine aircraft already on hand, commercial aviation was slow to introduce them. An economical interim engine was the turbo-prop, a hybrid prop jet that survives in short haul air transports. Finally, the British took the "pure" jet plunge in 1952 by putting into service the graceful De Havilland Comet. Two years later the plane had to be withdrawn after a series of tragic accidents which were caused by metal fatigue in the cabin. The commercial jet lead was assumed by the United States, where in 1958 the Boeing 707 was placed in service. A little over a year later nearly two and a half million passengers had flown them. The jet age had arrived.

Aviation's future is not tied to speed alone. The demand for short-distance, fast air transport to and from crowded airports has led to a profusion of STOL (Short Take Off and Landing) and VTOL (Vertical Take Off and Landing) designs. The need for greater payloads has produced still another new breed, the giant or "jumbo" jet, with a seating capacity for more than 500 passengers. The first of the new generation to go into scheduled airline service was the Boeing 747 in the fall of 1969.

Travel at supersonic speeds promises to come next. A rocket-driven experimental plane, the Bell X-1, broke the sound barrier (approximately 760 m.p.h. at sea level and 650 m.p.h. in the stratosphere) in 1947 by reaching Mach 1.07 (700 m.p.h.). The X-15 research airplane has since flown over 4,500 m.p.h. — more than six times the speed of sound. Since the 1950's, military jets produced by the leading nations routinely fly at supersonic speeds, pointing the way to a new future for commercial aviation. Already scheduled for commercial operation by 1971 is the joint French-British *Concorde* supersonic transport (SST), a Mach 2.2 design which made its first successful test hops early in 1969. The Soviet Union's entry in the SST field is the TU-144, which by the middle of 1969 was reported to have broken the sound barrier several times during test flights. The TU-144 was designed by Andrei Tupolev, the Soviet's leading aircraft designer.

91

The United States Supersonic Transport (SST)
when built will travel at speeds
of 1,800 miles per hour and have
a 300 to 350 passenger capacity

A larger and even faster SST is planned in the United States. This plane, the Boeing 733, is designed for speeds of Mach 2.7 (1,800 m.p.h.) with accommodations for 300 passengers. One of supersonic flight's many complex problems is achieving low takeoff and landing speeds in and out of airports. Other major problems are seen in such phenomena as supersonic boom and in high altitude, clear air turbulence (CAT). But SST engineers contend that like other seemingly insolvable problems throughout aviation history, these too will be overcome.

As an age of supersonic transports begins, a different kind of flight, this time to land man on another celestial body, has taken place. Man's first ventures into space have opened a new epoch of flight. The first tentative steps taken along these paths are the realization of our ancient yearning to know and understand the universe. Efforts toward this end began after World War II, when American and Soviet scientists, expanding upon the Germans' wartime rocket research, were able to devise a complex array of rocket-propelled missiles which could be applied to peaceful or military purposes. The most ambitious of their projects involved man's efforts to probe the vast expanse beyond the earth.

The Space Race between the United States and the U.S.S.R. opened with the Soviet's 1957 launching of Sputnik I, the first space vehicle to achieve orbit. A series of more sophisticated satellites followed, and in 1961 the U.S.S.R. put the first man, Major Yuri Gagarin, into orbit around the earth. The following year America had an astronaut of its own, Lieutenant Colonel John H. Glenn, circling the globe. By 1969 the landing of men on the Moon, the climactic event in America's Apollo series, had become a reality. As Neil Armstrong placed the first human foot on the surface of the Moon, he was heard to say, "That's one small step for man, one giant leap for mankind." But the Moon is only the first step toward outer space. The planets lie beyond, and some day man seems destined to visit them too.

Index